RESEARCH MONOGRAPHS OF THE NATIONAL ASSOCIATION
FOR THE EDUCATION OF YOUNG CHILDREN, VOLUME 3

Families and Early Childhood Programs

Douglas R. Powell

With a Foreword by Millie Almy

A 1988–1989 Comprehensive membership benefit

National Association for the Education of Young Children
Washington, D.C.

For Barbara, Rachel, and Philip

Photo credits: Subjects & Predicates *4, 18, 60, 66, 88, 92, 99, 114;* Elisabeth Nichols *7;* National Committee, Arts for the Handicapped, courtesy Very Special Arts *11;* Francis Wardle *25, 28;* Esther Mugar *34;* Sunrise/Trinity *38, 116;* Janice Mason *43;* Michael Tony-TOPIX *57;* Ginger Howard *73;* Nancy P. Alexander *81, 96;* Cleo Freelance Photo *111;* Marilyn Nolt *118.*

National Association for the Education of Young Children
1834 Connecticut Ave., N.W.
Washington, DC 20009-5786

The National Association for the Education of Young Children attempts through its publications program to provide a forum for discussion of major issues and ideas in our field. We hope to provoke thought and promote professional growth. The views expressed or implied are not necessarily those of the Association.

Library of Congress Catalog Card Number: 89-061025

ISBN 0-935989-22-6

NAEYC #142

Book design and production: Jack Zibulsky

Printed in the United States of America

Contents

Foreword

WHEN DOUGLAS POWELL ASKED ME to write a foreword for *Families and Early Childhood Programs,* the third in the series of annual Research Monographs recently begun by the National Association for the Education of Young Children, I was greatly pleased. One source of my pleasure lay in the realization that the series had become an actuality. The content of the monograph provided another source of satisfaction. Now, having read Powell's work, I also find delight in the way he has handled an important and exceedingly complex subject.

In establishing the annual research series parallel to the *Early Childhood Research Quarterly,* NAEYC has reaffirmed the tradition established some 60 years ago by its predecessor, the National Association for Nursery Education. At that time nursery school teachers were expected to base their programs on the emerging science of child development.

In the ensuing years the scientific knowledge about young children expanded tremendously. The number and diversity of the children increased to include poor and educationally disadvantaged children, disabled children, children for whom English was a second language, and, to an ever-increasing extent, infants and toddlers. The program of what came to be called the "traditional nursery school" took on new aspects to meet changing needs. In the face of these changing needs practitioners often found themselves lacking access to pertinent developmental literature. The annual Research Monograph series attempts to provide such access for issues that are of current and common concern. The *Early Childhood Research Quarterly* focuses even more directly on practice-oriented research.

As I look back over the more than 50 years in which I have been a participant in and observer of early childhood programs, I can think of no topic more relevant to the practitioner's ultimate success in promoting child development than the views about families she or he held. Such views were, and still are, epitomized in the interactions between teachers and parents. Who has power and authority and for what? Powell's discussion illuminates this issue and my experience confirms his position.

I did my student teaching and spent my first two years as a teacher in prestigious nursery schools in academic settings where child development research was carried on. Here the middle-class parents, many of them academic, appeared to accept the nursery school teachers as authorities on child development, particularly as it related to the nursery school program, where they were encouraged to be observers. If they had too many reservations about what they saw they could, as a matter of parental right, withdraw their child, whose place would be quickly taken by the next child on the waiting list. Such situations fitted nicely the then-current dictum that the nursery school "supplements and complements" parental child care but never supplants it. Clarity about parental power and authority as compared to that of the teachers became more elusive when I moved to a philanthropic day nursery that chose to incorporate early childhood education into its 12-hour child care program. When a mother's ability to earn her meager income is contingent on finding a safe place to leave her children, there can be little question about where the power lies. Interestingly, however, a number of parents sought guidance from teachers and director in ways that seemed not very different from those of the academic, middle-class parents I had known earlier.

Much the same can be said about parents in the Works Progress Administration (WPA) nursery schools of the Depression years, where parents were dependent on the program for their children's nutrition and health care. In contrast, parents in the Lanham Act Child Care Centers that replaced WPA nursery schools during World War II were not financially dependent. But their ability to earn, like that of the parents in the day nursery, depended on the availability of care.

In retrospect, I am impressed with two features of what has been called the first expansion of the nursery school movement. One feature relates to parents, the other to teachers.

A majority of parents in the WPA nursery schools and somewhat fewer in the Lanham Act Centers appeared very interested in and responsive to information from the science of child development. In the WPA nursery schools that I directed the parents met on a weekly basis with a parent educator who led them in, and sometimes taught them to lead, discussions on family problems; helped them to identify and use community resources; and in various ways provided support for their self-development and learning. These parent groups, coming from housing areas identified with different ethnic backgrounds, offered us evidence of cultural diversity and strengths that we did not then know how to build on. Parents in Lanham Act centers turned out in surprising numbers for brief meetings on topics of perennial concern, such as discipline, whenever the center provided a hot meal and child care. Unfortunately, as far as I am aware, no study of parents during this first expansion of nursery schools exists to substantiate my belief in the probable beneficial effects for parents.

What can be substantiated is that the expansion brought into the field many individuals who served as teachers but lacked solid backgrounds in child development. In-service training and further education on their own served to mitigate but did not fully change this situation. Whether it resulted in the lessening of the authority of the teachers is not known.

The second period of expansion, coming some 20 years after the first, began with programs for the disadvantaged, including Head Start. It continues as more and more parents need child care. Generally inadequate salaries and the greater availability of jobs for women and minorities in other fields have led to the necessity of again employing many practitioners with less than adequate backgrounds in child development.

NAEYC's recent emphasis on the professional aspects of the child care practitioner's work, its attempts to make the child development literature more accessible, as well as its increasing support for efforts to improve salaries and working conditions, are all steps toward clarifying and improving the role of the teachers vis-à-vis the parent. Such clarification seems essential if what has long been a slogan in the field, "parents as partners," is to be adequately realized.

It would be unfair to emphasize the importance of the teacher's access to the science of child development without pointing out that its literature has certain limitations. Although interdisciplinary approaches have been and continue to be essential, the bulk of the literature has been psychological. As Powell's discussion suggests, it is only recently that sociological perspectives have been given much consideration. Only recently, too, has the literature begun to deal with ethnic and class diversity without the implicit assumption that White, middle-class development is always to be emulated.

Powell has been able to cull and amplify the literature relating to parents and, more broadly, families to illuminate questions that perplex practitioners in today's early childhood programs. He notes appropriately that the field has often asserted the correctness of certain practices while lacking systematic evidence to support them. He also indicates that the theoretical grounds for strengthening the cooperation between families and early childhood programs is strong. It remains for practitioners and researchers to collaborate with one another, defining practices and investigating their appropriateness for specific field settings. From that, it seems, children, parents, and teachers all have much to gain.

Millie Almy

Chapter 1

Families and early childhood programs in a changing context

In THE PAST TWO DECADES, there has been a resurgence of interest in the role of the family in the care and education of young children. The current attention to family matters has two related strands. One stems from the dramatic growth of maternal participation in the labor force and the concomitant increase in the use of nonfamilial child care by middle-class families. This change in the American social landscape has prompted extensive debate about the integrity of the family and the wisdom of shared childrearing. The second strand represents growing concern about the ability of families to provide optimal childrearing environments in the context of widespread changes in the social fabric of families, neighborhoods, and communities. Adding to this concern is increased recognition of families' major influence on young children's social, emotional, and cognitive development. A consequence of the first strand is renewed calls for partnerships and continuity between families and early childhood programs, while the second strand has heightened interest in strategies to educate and support parents.

The themes of partnership, continuity, and parent education are familiar dimensions of the early childhood education field. Interest in home-school continuity long has been evident in preschool classroom practices. One of the goals of the Bank Street approach, for example, is to "alleviate conflict over separation related to loss of familiar context of place and people" (Biber, 1977, p. 443). Toward this end, the program recommends visits from home people to school, interchange of home and school objects, and school trips to home neighborhoods. An illustration of an interchange of home and school objects is a planned classroom experience in which children prepare and take home a small jar of applesauce for each family member, which Biber suggests "helps the child bridge the separation between home and school" (p. 451). The parent education theme also enjoys long-standing prominence in the field. The emphasis on parents in the settlement house movement of the 1880s, the nursery school movement of the 1920s, and the early intervention movement of the 1960s is exemplary of the parent participation tradition in early childhood education.

1

What differentiates the current era from earlier periods is the apparent permanence of out-of-home care and the profound change in the structural, cultural, and labor force characteristics of families.

Though not new in intensity or general focus, current interest in the family's childrearing role is an outgrowth of a vastly more complicated set of circumstances than encountered in previous periods of societal concern about the family. America has entered a new era of relations between families and early childhood programs that requires a reconsideration of the assumptions, goals, and methods of working with families. What differentiates the current era from earlier periods is the apparent permanence of shared childrearing with nonfamilial adults and institutions and the profound change in the structural, cultural, and labor force characteristics of families.

The apparent permanence of shared childrearing is especially significant because previous notable increases in the use of nonfamilial child care in the 20th Century have been in response to temporary needs of national versus individual origin. During World War II, for example, it was socially acceptable for women to enter the labor force because the country's war effort was deemed more important than mothers remaining at home to tend to children. The end of the war terminated the patriotic rationale for maternal employment, and there was a corresponding withdrawal of federal funds for child care (Fein & Clarke-Stewart, 1973). In the absence of an exceptional national emergency, the current use of out-of-home child care for the presumed purpose of satisfying parental self-interest is in conflict with core American ideologies regarding motherhood and the home as the best setting for young children.

The family demographic changes add a related yet different element of complexity. The conventional two-parent family, with father as sole wage earner, no longer represents the majority of users of early childhood programs. A superordinate challenge is to restructure program policies and practices to reflect the new realities of family structure, lifestyle, and ethnic characteristics. Unfortunately, the knowledge gained from the experiences and research of earlier eras is of limited use in guiding responses to the current situation.

This monograph appears at a time when there is a need to assess critically what we know from research and theory about relations between families and early childhood programs, and the operations and effectiveness of parent education and support programs. The monograph has been organized toward this end. Its primary purpose is to review existing empirical and theoretical knowledge in an effort to clarify pressing issues and point to needed directions in practice and research.

This introductory chapter provides a framework for the volume by: setting forth the major rationales for working with parents; describing recent developments regarding relations between families and early child-

*The doctrine of parental rights to go along with parental
responsibilities is a core American value.*

hood programs; and identifying persistent and contemporary problems
confronting the early childhood field regarding relations with families.

Chapter 2 examines research and theoretical perspectives on continuity
between families and early childhood programs. Most recommended practices and rationales regarding program-family collaboration stem from
concern about the continuity of children's socialization experiences. Chapter 2 considers three prevailing assumptions about program-family continuity. In Chapter 3, the nature and effects of relations between parents and
early childhood programs are examined. Attention is given to a variety of
early childhood programs. Chapter 4 reviews research on the methods and
effects of programs that attempt to enhance the childrearing role of
families with young children. Both home- and center-based programs are
included. Promising directions for program practices and research are
suggested in Chapter 5.

Major premises and anticipated outcomes

Major premises

Three premises about families and society constitute the foundation of
most arguments for early childhood programs and families to form and
maintain close working relations, and for efforts to enhance the family's
childrearing role.

Doctrine of parental rights. This doctrine is a core American value.
The responsibility for determining the child's best interest has rested first
and foremost with parents (Coons & Sugarman, 1978). The dramatic
increase in the use of nonfamilial child care has prompted concern that
secondary institutions might replace families as the primary childrearing
system. President Nixon's veto of the Mondale-Brademas child development bill in 1971 was indicative of this concern. Nixon noted the undesir-
ability of "communal approaches to child rearing," which work "against
the family-centered approach" (Nixon, 1971, pp. S21129–S21130).

More recent legislative reminders of parental rights in early education
programs are the Education of All Handicapped Children Act (Public Law
94-142) of 1975 and the Education of the Handicapped Act Amendments
(Public Law 99-457) of 1986. Both laws require parental involvement in
decisions about a child's educational placement and treatment plan. Another recent example is Executive Order 12606, signed by President
Reagan on September 2, 1987, which calls for all executive departments

Educators have long acknowledged the significant influence of the family on the care and education of the child.

and agencies to consider the impact on families of current policies and regulations as well as proposed regulatory and statutory provisions. One of the criteria for assessing the impact of federal policies on families asks, "Does this action strengthen or erode the authority and rights of parents in the education, nurture, and supervision of their children?" (Section 1b).

Teachers or caregivers have authority over children by virtue of parental extension or delegation of parental authority. The parental rights doctrine has contributed to a view of the parent as *de facto guardian* who selects a preschool program that ensures support of family values (Fein, 1980). This doctrine underlies arguments for maximizing parental choice and the range of early childhood programs available.

Familial influences of the child. Educators have long acknowledged the significant influence of the family on the care and education of the child. Years ago, Pestalozzi (1747–1827) argued that, for children, "the teaching of their parents will always be the core" and that the role of the

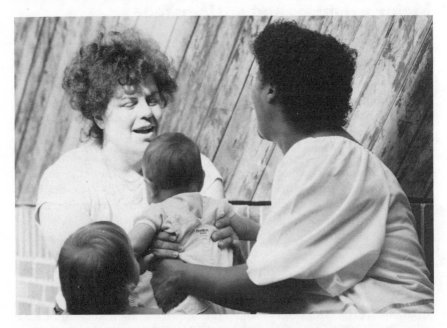

Home-school continuity has positive effects on the child: Goals for children are best achieved if the important adults in their lives agree on and are consistent about the way they deal with children. Parent-teacher cooperation facilitates a child's separation from home and entry into a new child care setting.

Parent participation is consistent with the value system of a democratic society. For example, the Economic Opportunity Act of 1964 called for "maximum feasible participation" of individuals served by community action programs.

teacher is to provide a "decent shell" around the core (Pestalozzi, 1951, p. 26). Research studies in the 1960s and 1970s fueled this belief by concluding that family variables were more powerful than school variables in predicting academic performance (Coleman et al., 1966; Jencks et al., 1972).

Recognition of the family as the child's primary socialization agent has been accompanied by periodic calls for monitoring parental performance (Caldwell, 1980; Anastasiow, 1988) and by recommendations for providing parents with childrearing information and guidance. It has been argued, for instance, that every child deserves a trained parent (Rheingold, 1973; Bell, 1975). All theories of child development hold that lay persons need expert guidance in the rearing of young children (Kessen, 1979). This spirit is embodied in a proposal from Honig (1979) for a Parent's Bill of Rights that includes access to knowledge about child development and child observation skills.

Acknowledgment of the family's role as a major socialization force also has contributed to the notion that preschool experiences must be reinforced at home if the preschool is to have long-term impact on the child.

Democratic processes. The principle of parent participation is consistent with the value system of a democratic society. This principle received renewed interest with the Economic Opportunity Act of 1964, which called for "maximum feasible participation" of individuals served by community action programs. This legislation extended the spirit of citizen involvement in democratic processes to programs for low-income populations, as reflected in the placement of parents in program decision-making roles in Head Start. Outcomes of parental participation in decision-making roles were anticipated in two areas: self-development (i.e., competence) and institutional sensitivity.

Illustrative of the participation principle is the experience of an early Head Start program that implemented the innovative idea of having an educational program for a poor Black community run by the people themselves. In the Child Development Group of Mississippi program, the guiding framework was that

> [citizens] would learn how to run their own programs though participating in the running of every step and phase of the program. If efforts weren't made to find out who had interest in this, and efforts weren't made to be patient with that mild interest and fan it, the usual thing would happen. Because poor people were *not* making decisions, other people *would be* making decisions. We would have missed the essence of the poverty program: to reduce the helplessness people feel about their own fate. (Greenberg, 1969, p. 45)

Parent participation has been viewed as a means of fostering the growth and development of parents as people.

Anticipated outcomes

Arguments for working with families of young children often are based on anticipated effects. Four outcome areas can be discerned from the literature and are briefly noted below. Subsequent chapters examine the existing theoretical and research evidence regarding these four areas.

1. *Child competence.* The prevailing theme of discussions about program-family relations is that goals for children are best achieved if the important adults in their lives agree on and are consistent about the way they deal with children. A related theme is that parent-teacher cooperation facilitates a child's separation from home and entry into a new child care setting. The underlying assumption is that home-school continuity has positive effects on the child.

This anticipated outcome is a basis of recommendations for

- frequent sharing of home and school information between parents and teachers;
- parents to accompany and spend time with their child in a new early childhood setting;
- parental involvement in program decision making that contributes to program sensitivity to family values and characteristics;
- parents to learn about child development; and
- maximizing parental choice in the selection of preschool programs that are congruent with family values.

The expectation of improved child competence is also a rationale for providing education support programs to help families rear young children. Increases in academic performance and cognitive skills, and reductions in the incidence of child abuse and neglect, typically are promoted as the desired benefits of education and support programs aimed at parents.

2. *Parents' self-development.* Parent participation has been viewed as a means of fostering the growth and development of parents as people. It has been anticipated that involvement in preschool programs would enhance parents' feelings of self-worth and contribute to the development or refinement of job-related skills. Control over one's destiny in a program is seen as a mechanism for helping individuals improve their feeling of competence (Zigler & Berman, 1983) and pursue productive, contributing roles in the larger society (Valentine & Stark, 1979).

M. Brewster Smith's (1968) theoretical work on the origins of competence is exemplary of the conceptual framework used to justify participation, especially among low-income and ethnic minority populations (see Chilman, 1973). Smith argued that attitudes of hope and of self-respect are

Concerns about ways to monitor and maintain the quality of nonfamilial care contribute to the argument that parents can improve the quality of care through their roles as informed consumers.

*One early rationale for parent participation in Head Start
was that involvement in program decision making would be
a beginning political step toward changing human service
institutions.*

the crux of competence and that an individual's location in the social
structure influences the development of competence through the provision of opportunity, respect, and power. According to Smith, "When
opportunities are offered without a sharing of power, we have paternalism,
which undercuts respect [and] accentuates dependence . . ." (p. 313).

3. *Human service institutions (including child care).* Parent participation in early childhood programs has been justified as a strategy for
improving human service institutions. For parents of all economic strata,
participation in their child's program has been viewed as experiential
training for dealing with personnel and practices in schools and other
institutions that may be insensitive to constituent interests and needs.

One of the early rationales for parent participation in Head Start was
that involvement in program decision making would be a beginning
political step toward changing human service institutions. This idea was
part of a larger plan to eradicate poverty by giving the poor a modicum
of political power that eventually could be used to change social institutions that perpetuated poverty by denying access to resources such as
jobs and adequate education (Valentine & Stark, 1979). Thus, parent
participation has been viewed as a mechanism for social change (Moore &
McKinley, 1972).

Parents also have been seen as a vehicle for improving the quality of
child care in this country. The rapid expansion of child care in the 1970s
and 1980s, and concomitant concerns about ways to monitor and maintain the quality of nonfamilial care, contributed to the argument that
parents can improve the quality of care through their roles as *informed
consumers* (Levine, 1982). By learning the indicators of child care quality
(Bradbard & Endsley, 1980) as well as directly experiencing high-quality
care, it is thought, parents can exert influence on quality through their
consumer behavior in the child care marketplace.

4. *Program resources.* Lastly, parent participation has been promoted
as a means to garner additional resources for early childhood programs
through parents' roles as volunteers in service delivery, as advocates for
increased societal support of children's programs, and as fund raisers.

Overview of recent developments

In recent years there has been an overwhelming level of activity that
directly or indirectly attempts to put into operation one or more of the
preceding premises. The following description of recent developments is
not an exhaustive portrayal of the extent and scope of the numerous and

This idea was part of a larger plan to gradually give the poor a modicum of political power to change the social institutions that perpetuate poverty by denying access to resources such as jobs and adequate education.

diverse activities. The intent is to highlight major accomplishments and trends indicative of the escalating interest in relations between families and early childhood programs and in the childrearing environments of families. The developments are organized into three areas: practice guidelines; federal, state and local initiatives; and emphasis on family support.

Practice guidelines. The 1980s have been marked by the appearance of several thoughtful statements about appropriate relations between families and programs. No national professional organization has developed standards for the design and implementation of high-quality parent education and support programs, but indexes of quality have been proposed (see Chapter 4 and Powell, 1988c).

The standards of professional practice in early childhood programs developed by the National Association for the Education of Young Children include staff-parent interaction as a component of a high-quality program. The National Academy of Early Childhood Programs uses these standards to accredit programs for young children. A premise of the staff-parent interaction component is that "programs cannot adequately meet the needs of children unless they also recognize the importance of the child's family and develop strategies to work effectively with families" (National Academy of Early Childhood Programs, 1984, p. 15). The standards call for parents to be well informed about the program and welcome as observers and contributors. Further, the standards specify that staff-parent interaction in high-quality early childhood programs should include the following:

1. Information about the program is given to new and prospective families, including written descriptions of the program's philosophy and operating procedures. . . .

2. A process has been developed for orienting children and parents to the center which may include a pre-enrollment visit, parent orientation meeting, or gradual introduction of children to the center. . . .

3. Staff and parents communicate regarding home and center childrearing practices in order to minimize potential conflicts and confusion for children. . . .

4. Parents are welcome as visitors in the center at all times (for example, to observe, eat lunch with a child, or volunteer to help in the classroom). Parents and other family members are encouraged to be involved in the program in various ways, taking into consideration working parents and those with little spare time.

5. A verbal and/or written system is established for sharing day-to-day happenings that may affect children. Changes in a child's physical or emotional state are regularly reported. (pp. 15–16)

Parent participation has garnered additional resources for early childhood programs through parents' roles as volunteers in service delivery, as advocates for increased societal support of children's programs, and as fund raisers.

The National Black Child Development Institute (NBCDI) includes parent involvement as one of the 10 "safeguards" or guidelines for establishing child development programs for 4-year-olds in the public schools (National Black Child Development Institute, 1987). The NBCDI calls for public school early childhood programs to involve parents in decisions about curriculum and program policy. Specific suggestions include a standing parent committee to work with teachers surrounding curriculum matters and an active role for parents in periodic evaluations of program operations.

Federal, state, and local initiatives. Initiatives aimed at strengthening the family's childrearing competence have dominated early childhood program development activity in the past two decades at federal, state, and local levels.

Head Start, this nation's most extensive investment in the education of young children, has experimented with and refined strategies for involving families in program activities since its inception in 1965 (Zigler & Freedman, 1987). The "maximum feasible participation" of parents in program decisions and operations was integral to the original Head Start plans. Since 1970 the Head Start Policy Manual has mandated performance standards for four areas of parent participation:

1. participation in making decisions about the nature and operation of the program;

2. participation in the classroom as paid employees, volunteers, or observers;

3. activities for the parents that they have helped to develop; and

4. working with their children in cooperation with the staff of the center.

In 1987, a national Task Force on Parent Involvement in Head Start, commissioned by the federal government's Administration for Children, Youth and Families, issued a report on ways to strengthen parent involvement in Head Start nationwide. The report has 38 recommendations, paying specific attention to these four areas of parent participation. Furthermore, in the 1970s Head Start developed several program models that approached parents as the primary recipient of services: Home Start, the Parent Child Centers, and the Child and Family Resource Program.

The recent Education of the Handicapped Act Amendments (Public Law 99-457), which provide assistance to states in offering early intervention services for infants and toddlers and their families, contain provisions for significant involvement of families. The law stipulates that a multidisciplinary team that includes the parent or guardian develop an individual-

In the past two decades, initiatives aimed at strengthening the family's childrearing competence have dominated early childhood program development at federal, state, and local levels.

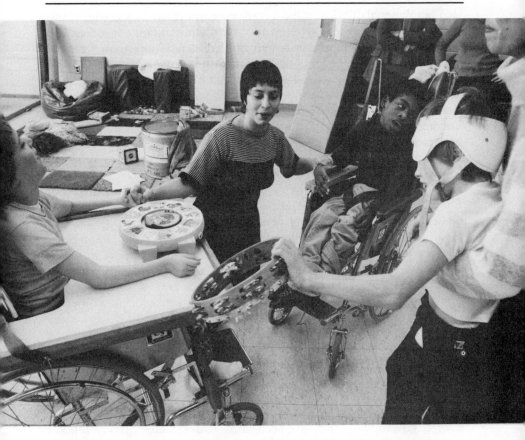

Public laws 94–142 and 99–457 contain provisions for significant involvement of families.

Efforts are underway to encourage public school programs for young children to be more responsive to families.

ized family service plan that has a statement of the family's strengths and needs in enhancing the development of the disabled infant or toddler. The family, then, is a focus of service delivery. This legislation strengthens the commitment to parent involvement set forth in Public Law 94-142, the Education of All Handicapped Children Act of 1975. This law mandates parents to participate with professionals in the development of an individualized educational program (IEP) for their children and enables parents to initiate a hearing if they do not agree with the diagnosis of the child, the placement, and/or the IEP.

Efforts also are underway to encourage public school programs for young children to be more responsive to families (see Kagan, 1987). The Early Childhood Task Force of the National Association of State Boards of Education recently issued a report, titled *Right From the Start,* that focuses on school reform in the early years of education (through age 8). The report calls for elementary schools to establish early childhood units that "launch new plans for parental outreach and family support in which parents are valued as primary influences in the children's lives and are essential partners in their education" (Schultz & Lombardi, 1989, p. 8). The new federal Even Start initiative, a family-centered education program authorized as part of Chapter 1 of Title 1 of Public Law 100-297, provides funds to local educational agencies for programs that help parents become full partners in their children's education and to assist children in reaching their full potentials as learners. Program elements include instructional programs that promote adult literacy and prepare parents to support their children's educational growth. Home-based programs are one of the outreach mechanisms.

State governments also have been active in developing early childhood initiatives focused on families (Weiss & Seppanen, 1988). One of the oldest state-funded efforts is Minnesota's Early Childhood and Family Education program, founded in 1975. Operated through local school districts, this program provides parent group discussions, home visits, child development classes, and other approaches to enhancing and supporting the competence of parents in providing an environment for healthy child development. Parents constitute the majority membership of each local program advisory board. Other state-level initiatives include Parents as Teachers in Missouri, the Ounce of Prevention Fund in Illinois, Family Support Centers in Maryland, Parent Education and Support Centers in Connecticut, and the Parent Child Education Program in Kentucky.

Recently, large cities and smaller communities have developed and implemented a variety of locally initiated programs that focus on parents of young children or include a systematic effort to involve families in early

State governments have been active in developing early childhood initiatives focused on families.

childhood programs. Examples are **Family Focus,** a drop-in center approach to family support in the Chicago area (Weissbourd, 1987); **MELD,** a long-term peer support group strategy for first-time parents based in Minneapolis (Ellwood, 1988); **Avance,** a comprehensive San Antonio, Texas, parent support program involving Mexican-American families with very young children (Rodriquez & Cortez, 1988); and New York City's **Giant Step,** an educational program for 4-year-old children that has a family worker for each of the classrooms (New York City Mayor's Office of Early Childhood Education, 1987–88).

Emphasis on family support. Largely in response to the work of Urie Bronfenbrenner (1979) and to changes in family demographic characteristics, there has been a good deal of interest in the social ecology of child development and parenthood. This has resulted in a burgeoning of research and program activity surrounding family support systems (e.g., Kagan, Powell, Weissbourd, & Zigler, 1987; Gottlieb, 1988). A focus on the family context is now evident in descriptions of child care programs as well as parent education and support programs.

Conceptualizations of child care as a family support system have been increasingly prevalent in the past two decades. For example, Caldwell (1985) has suggested that a high-quality child care program functions as an extended family, and a pioneering descriptive study of exemplary child care programs was titled *The New Extended Family: Day Care That Works* (Galinsky & Hooks, 1977). Data that suggest that the quality (e.g., stability) of a child care arrangement is a significant predictor of parents' performance in the work setting (i.e., absenteeism and unproductive time) lend support to the notion that the effects of child care extend well beyond the child (Galinsky, 1986).

Most early childhood intervention programs established in the 1960s and 1970s included a major parent involvement component (e.g., the Perry Preschool Project; see Weikart, Bond, & McNeil, 1978), but in the 1980s many early intervention programs broadened the focus on parents to include family support. For instance, the Family, Infant and Preschool Program of the Western Carolina Center has evolved from a child-focused early intervention program to a family-systems-oriented program, serving disabled and developmentally at-risk children (Dunst & Trivette, 1988). This shift represents an emerging direction in the early intervention field wherein the social context of parenthood, including interactions between the family and its larger social environment, is a target of change (Powell, 1988a). Environmental influences on family functioning such as housing, employment, extended family relations, and health care are among the areas of interest in intervention programs focusing on the ecology of family life.

Many locally initiated programs focus on parents of young children or include a systematic effort to involve families in early childhood programs.

The family resource movement of the 1980s also is evidence of a growing focus on the provision of programmatic support for families with young children (see Weissbourd, 1983; Kagan et al., 1987). Key assumptions of this movement are:

- all families need support regardless of economic status or specific concerns;
- personal social networks are a major source of support for families;
- the provision of social support during the first years of a child's life serves a preventive function; and
- support to families should make use of existing community resources (Family Resource Coalition, 1981).

The Family Resource Coalition, based in Chicago, was founded in 1981 by community-based, grassroots programs as a national organization to promote the development of family support programs through information dissemination, advocacy, and technical assistance.

Persistent and contemporary problems

In an effort to provide a framework for this monograph, this chapter has identified the premises and anticipated outcomes of work with parents and described some recent developments indicative of the growing interest in the role of families in the care and education of young children. This last section sets forth three dominant problems in the current context of families and early childhood programs: changes in family characteristics, imprecise definitions and contrasting images of parent participation, and concerns among teachers regarding relations with parents.

Changing family characteristics

The dramatic changes in the characteristics of American families in the past three decades are well known to seasoned early childhood professionals. Variations among families currently using early childhood programs are markedly greater than the differences among families using preschool programs in earlier eras. Early childhood educators increasingly serve families characterized by single-parent households, cultural diversity and ethnic minority status, dual-worker or dual-career lifestyles, reconstituted ("blended") family arrangements, struggles with real or perceived

Intervention programs focusing on the ecology of family life address influences such as housing, employment, extended family relations, and health care.

economic pressures, and geographic mobility that decreases access to support traditionally available from extended family members.

More than family demographic changes may be occurring in America with regard to the care and education of young children. James Coleman (1987) has argued that over the past 25 years there has been an extensive erosion of *social capital* within families and communities for the proper rearing of children. In the family, social capital includes the presence of adults and the range of parent-child exchanges about academic, social, and personal matters. In the community, social capital involves norms of social control, adult-sponsored youth organizations, and informal relations between adults and children that permit, for instance, an adult lending a sympathetic ear to problems not discussible with parents. Another indication of this erosion is society's advance of individualism, wherein concern for one's own well-being supersedes interest in others. There is evidence that Americans' sense of collective responsibility for other people's children has deteriorated in recent years (Halpern, 1987). These radical changes in family characteristics present challenges to early childhood professionals in at least three areas: (1) increasingly parents are unlikely to be available for traditional modes of parent participation in program activities; (2) the content of preschool and elementary school classrooms assumes a level of quality in children's family-based socialization experiences that may not be provided by growing numbers of families at all economic levels; (3) educators are increasingly called upon to develop appropriate responses to families from cultural and linguistic minority backgrounds. A look at each of these areas follows.

Availability of parents to support program activities. The new demographics of family structure and function prompt questions about the viability of existing approaches to relations between families and early childhood programs. Some scholars have argued that today's practices of working with parents are based on yesterday's idealized images of the nuclear family. For instance, Heath and McLaughlin (1987) claim that both dual-career and single-parent families "have precious little time or energy to spend working as partners in their children's education, visiting the school, attending conferences, or providing extracurricular activities for their children" (p. 578).

Data on this topic are limited. Clearly the significant numbers of mothers in the paid work force and welfare reform policies that require out-of-home work potentially reduce the pool of parents available for center-based activities. Research examining the relation of program partici-

The dominant assumption of many teachers is that parents are unable or unwilling to assist with school-related activities.

pation to parents' work status and family responsibilities seem nonexistent in the early childhood field. At the elementary school level, a questionnaire survey of 1,269 parents in 82 first, third, and fifth grade Maryland classrooms found that 42% of parents not active at school worked outside the home during school hours (Epstein, 1986). Others had small children, family problems, or other activities that demanded their time. Twelve percent reported they had not been asked to assist at school.

For home-based activities with children, however, the Maryland findings offer a story that conflicts with the image of parents as too busy to assist their child with school work. Epstein found that only 8% of the parents reported they never helped their child with reading and math work during the school year, regardless of teacher requests. Over 85% of the respondents reportedly spent 15 minutes or more helping their children on homework activities when asked to do so by the teacher. Moreover, most parents indicated that they could help more (up to an average of 44 minutes) if the teacher gave direction on what to do. Single parents reported spending more minutes helping their child at home than did married parents, but indicated they did not have sufficient time to do all the teacher expected (Epstein, 1984b, 1985).

Nonetheless, the dominant assumption of many teachers is that parents are unable or unwilling to assist with school-related activities. In the Maryland study, more than half (56%) of the 82 classrooms had teachers who did not emphasize parent involvement activities. These teachers believed that parents lacked the ability or willingness to work with their child (Becker & Epstein, 1982). One teacher in this study said, "Parents are so involved with staying alive and being able to keep up economically, there is little or no energy left to devote to children. . . . Many of the children I teach are too busy raising the little children in the family, cleaning house, and doing adult work at home because their parents are out trying to make ends meet" (Epstein & Becker, 1982, p. 111).

Quality of family-based socialization. One result of the reduction in social capital, according to Coleman, is that many families at all social levels do not provide an environment that enables children to benefit from schools as they currently exist. The crux of Coleman's argument is that families and other intimate environments close to the child provide unique inputs into the socialization process in the form of attitudes, effort, and conception of self. In contrast, formal institutions of childrearing such as schools and child care centers are structured to provide a different set of

Interaction of the resources the family devotes to a child's education with the resources provided by the school contributes to academic performance.

socialization inputs, loosely described as opportunities, demands, and rewards. Coleman's research suggests that the *interaction* of these two sets of inputs contributes to academic performance; that is, the resources devoted by the family to a child's education interact with the resources provided by the school. The well-known Equality of Educational Opportunity report (Coleman et al., 1966) demonstrated that variations among family backgrounds make more difference in achievement than do variations among schools. Schools are more effective for children from strong family backgrounds than for children from resource-weak families. Coleman argues that the reduction of social capital in families and communities should not be replaced, then, with more school-like resources but with experiences that approximate the qualities traditionally provided by home and community.

Responses to cultural diversity. The rapidly growing cultural diversity in America presents crucial challenges to designers and staff of programs aimed at ethnic minority families (Washington & Oyemade, 1985). The existing research literature contains little information about appropriate methods of parent education and support for cultural and linguistic minority populations. What types of staff roles, delivery systems, and program content are likely to be culturally responsive to the interests and characteristics of different populations?

With regard to early childhood programs for children from low-income and ethnic minority families, it has been argued that home-school discontinuities present major conflicts that contribute to poor school achievement (Baratz & Baratz, 1970; Ramirez & Castañeda, 1974). Laosa (1982) has proposed that home and school engage in a process of mutual adaptation to eliminate incompatibilities between the two environments and produce *articulated continuity* between them. He suggests that social competence involves functional adaptations to more than one environment and that a child's success in two different environments may depend on the extent of overlap of the characteristic demands of the two settings. Laosa's paradigm calls for no culture or subculture to be superior to others and for children to be exposed to experiences that foster biculturalism, resulting in the acquisition of two parallel sets of competencies that enable the child to function effectively in both settings. Again, the existing literature is sparse in terms of delineating specific home-school linkage strategies that might fulfill Laosa's plan.

The rapidly growing cultural diversity in America presents crucial challenges to designers and staff of programs aimed at ethnic minority families.

Lack of consensus in the field about the operational meaning of partnership and similar labels allows for enormous variation in the way similar or identical labels are put into operation.

Imprecise definitions and contrasting images of parental roles

Work with families in the early childhood education field reflects diverse images of parental roles vis-à-vis program participation and uses a variety of imprecise labels to characterize different methods or approaches. As a consequence, professional communication in the field is seriously hampered, and conceptual and programmatic advances are difficult to realize. It is impossible, for instance, to answer the question, "What are the effects of parent participation in early childhood programs?" without a clear understanding of what is entailed in the "parent participation" term.

The concept of *partnership* typically is evoked to prescribe and describe the nature of relations between parents and program staff. The notion is that parents and teachers represent major influences on the child that need to be coordinated through collaborative relations. Other labels frequently used to portray the program-family connection include *parent involvement, parent participation,* and *parent-teacher collaboration.* A distinctively different image of the parent role is emerging in relation to the view of child care as a service industry: parents as *consumers or customers.* This role seems to be implied in the following message found on an advertisement for a day care information service aimed at child care administrators: "Do you know when parents are most likely to pull kids from your day-care program?" The advertisement promises to send subscribers a free report on "How to Keep Parents Happy after Enrollment."

There is no consensus in the field about the operational meaning of partnership and similar labels, and hence there is the potential for enormous variation in the way similar or identical labels are put into operation. For some programs, parent participation may mean one-way communication, from program to parent, via written announcements and lectures. For other programs, the concept may represent a relatively equal flow of information and influence between program and family. The 25-year experience of Head Start in attempting to define and implement the parent participation label is representative of the field's lack of a precise concept (Valentine & Stark, 1979).

The lack of precise definitions and the resultant potential for conflicting interpretations partly is a function of unresolved tensions in the field about the extent to which programs should accommodate parental interests. As discussed in Chapters 3 and 5, direct parental influence on decisions regarding program philosophy and operations is problematic in the educational and human services, including early childhood.

Existing evidence suggests the parent-teacher relationship may be one of the more difficult aspects of work with young children.

The definition and interpretation problem also represents a legacy of ambivalent stances in the field about the extent to which parents possess strengths and interests in children that are worthy of equal status with program staff. One view is that parents (primarily mothers) lack the personal resources and/or desire to provide an appropriately stimulating environment for optimal child development. The deficiencies may be a result of personal (e.g., disposition) or environmental (e.g., inadequate housing and income) factors. The typical response is to place the child in a program that will *compensate* for the deficiencies of the home and to implement strategies to bolster parental resources and/or interest in childrearing. Threads of this image exist in the history of both the child care (Fein & Clarke-Stewart, 1973) and the early childhood intervention (Baratz & Baratz, 1970) movements in this country. An alternative view is that all parents possess strengths for rearing young children that deserve recognition and encouragement (e.g., Cochran, 1988a; Lally, Mangione, & Honig, 1988). Traces of *this* image, also, exist in the history of nursery education and early childhood education. Within this paradigm, collaboration with parents is based on mutual respect and a desire to empower parents with information and roles that strengthen control of the environment.

Parents and teachers: "Natural enemies"?

More than a half century ago, Willard Waller (1932) observed that parents and teachers are "natural enemies" (p. 68). The basis of his argument was that parents and teachers maintain qualitatively different relationships with the same child, especially in regard to affective bonds and spheres of responsibility, and as a consequence want different things for the child. While some may consider Waller's idea of enemy status to be an overstatement, existing evidence suggests the parent-teacher relationship may be one of the more difficult aspects of work with young children (Almy, 1982).

A professional ethics survey conducted of *Young Children* readers found that relationships with parents were the greatest area of ethical concern among early childhood educators at all job categories (teacher, administrator, etc.). Forty-seven percent of the nearly 600 respondents indicated ethical concerns about issues surrounding staff-parent relations. The most prevalent ethical issues about parents were in the areas of child abuse and neglect, referrals to outside agencies, and divorce and custody (Feeney & Sysko, 1986).

Teachers in their first years of teaching report difficulties in relating to parents. In a review of 83 studies of the perceived problems of beginning teachers in elementary and secondary schools, relations with parents emerged as the fifth most frequently mentioned problem (Veenman, 1984). Teachers disliked the parents' insufficient support for their ideas and parents' inadequate interest in the well-being of their children at school. Also, beginning teachers believed parents lacked confidence in their competence. The findings of one observational study included in the review suggested that parents placed pressure on beginning elementary teachers through phone calls and comments made during visits to the school (McIntosh, 1977). (The other top four perceived problems of beginning teachers in the Veenman review were: classroom discipline, motivating students, dealing with individual differences, and assessing student's work.)

These findings are consistent with anecdotal reports of teachers expressing negative perceptions of the level of parents' interest in their child. Consider the following voices of teachers: "[Parents] want a high-quality program for as cheap a price as possible and would like to drop off their children tomorrow!" "I think they'd [parents] be willing to leave the children here all day and all night, and I don't know if they'd even call" (Galinsky, 1988, p. 4).

Summary

This chapter has argued that dramatic changes in the structural, cultural, and labor force characteristics of families and the concomitant apparent permanence of shared childrearing arrangements are primary contributors to the current widespread interest in the role of the family in care and education of young children. These changes have led to renewed calls for partnerships between families and early childhood programs and have stimulated the development of programs to support the family's childrearing role. Though the themes of partnership and family support are not new to the early childhood field, the current family forms, functions, and lifestyles present challenges not previously addressed by the field in an extensive manner.

Three major premises serve as rationales for programmatic work with families: the doctrine of parental rights; familial influences on child development; and the principles of democratic participation. Potential benefits of work with families include improved child competence, parents' self-development, increased responsiveness of human service programs (e.g., public schools), and increased resources for early childhood programs.

The field's emerging responses to a changing social context include the appearance of practice guidelines for working with parents; ambitious family-oriented initiatives at federal, state, and local levels; and changes in existing programs for young children that reflect a conceptual and operational emphasis on the family. While these developments appear promising, there are new as well as persistent critical problems the field needs to address. One problem area pertains to the implications of the new family demographics for (a) parental availability for traditional modes of program participation, (b) program assumptions about the quality of children's socialization experiences in the home, and (c) program responsiveness to cultural diversity, including ethnic minorities. A second problem is the lack of precise definitions and generally accepted assumptions regarding the concept and practice of parent participation in program operations. Lastly, there are indications in the literature that some early childhood teachers find work with parents to be a source of tension.

Chapter 2

From the perspective of children: Continuity between families and early childhood programs

CONCERN ABOUT THE CONTINUITY of children's experiences is a central rationale for most strategies aimed at strengthening relations between families and early childhood programs. Three underlying assumptions are operating here: (1) Discontinuities exist between families and nonfamilial early childhood settings; (2) discontinuities may have negative effects on children (and, conversely, continuity between settings is beneficial to children); and (3) communication between parents and early childhood program staff can increase the level of continuity between home and program(s). These assumptions are inherent in the commonly recommended practice of encouraging parents to provide teachers with information that will help the teacher develop realistic goals and respond to the child in ways that acknowledge family circumstances (e.g., Hess & Croft, 1981). These assumptions also are a driving force in the practice of disseminating program and child development information to parents in the hope that parents will reinforce and extend the ideologies and practices of the early childhood program (e.g., Powell & Stremmel, 1987). The overriding expectation, then, is that progam responsiveness to home-related issues and parental responsiveness to program-related issues will result in greater continuity of program-home experience for the child, with corresponding benefits for the child.

Serious consideration of the argument that children benefit from close relations between socialization agencies requires an examination of the nature and effects on children of continuity and discontinuity between home and preschool program. Specifically, what is the theoretical and research base of recommendations for home-school relations that emphasize the continuity of children's experiences across settings? This chapter addresses three major questions: To what extent do discontinuities exist between families and early childhood programs? What are the effects of continuity/discontinuity on children? What is the effect on children of efforts to strengthen connections between families and early childhood programs? The chapter concludes with summary of what we know and do

Continuity has been treated in a global and dichotomous fashion, with little attention to the conditions under which continuity/discontinuity is beneficial or harmful.

---

not know from research about the nature and effects on children of program-family continuity. The final section also assesses the adequacy of the theoretical and empirical base recommendations to strengthen relations between families and early childhood programs.

The term *continuity* is used frequently in the early childhood field but unfortunately has not been well defined. Peters and Kontos (1987) note that the terms *continuity of care, continuum of services, environmental consistency, developmental continuity, continuity of supportive parenting,* and *contextual stability* are often used without definition and in a manner that suggests they are synonymous. As a result, continuity has been treated in a global and dichotomous fashion, with little attention to the conditions under which continuity/discontinuity is beneficial or harmful.

In this monograph, continuity refers to *linkages* and *congruence* between families and early childhood programs. Linkages include the level and type of communication between home and program, and the frequency with which members of one setting are present in the other setting (e.g., teacher visits home; parents visit program). Congruence refers to the degree of program-family similarity to childrearing values, goals, expectations, language codes, and the nature of adult-child interactions and relationships. Linkages deal with *structural* aspects of the program-family relationship, while congruence pertains to the *substance* of activities and exchanges within a setting. Chapter 5 discusses relationships between linkage and congruence dimensions of program-family continuity, including the relative merits of targeting linkage and/or congruence in strategies to improve continuity between home and early childhood program.

To what extent do discontinuities exist?

Theoretical perspectives

Sociological analyses of relations between families and nonfamilial socialization agencies indicate that certain types of discontinuity between settings are inevitable, given the unique properties of bureaucracies (i.e., child care centers, schools) and primary groups (i.e., families). Achievement, specialization, and impersonal relations are emphasized in most bureaucracies, while the norm of interpersonal relations in most primary groups is love and positive affect. Bureaucracies tend to focus on a few goals with specialists, while primary groups generally stress multiple goals and require generalized concern with each (Litwak & Meyer, 1974).

Child care providers envision their setting to be more akin to a primary group than a bureaucracy, with adult-child exchanges more closely approximating the parent-child relationship than a teacher-child relationship.

CONTINUITY — FROM THE PERSPECTIVE OF CHILDREN/25

Consider the value code differences confronted by a child in a classroom that emphasizes delayed gratification but whose family experiences focus on basic survival.

These setting differences are manifest in the roles assumed by teachers and parents. Katz (1980) has set forth theoretical distinctions between mothering and teaching in such areas as attachment level, intensity of affect, degree of spontaneity, and scope of responsibility. For instance, Katz proposed that mothers should be as spontaneous as possible with their children whereas teachers should strive to maintain predetermined goals and objectives. As another example, optimum attachment is necessary in the mother-child relationship whereas optimum detachment should characterize teacher-child relationships so as to permit objective appraisal of the child and to avoid emotional burnout of the teacher. Anna Freud's (1952) observation is apropos here: If teachers "play the part of a mother, we get from the child the reactions which are appropriate for the mother-child relationship" (p. 231).

Whether these setting differences exist in situations where the early childhood program views itself operationally as an extention of the family is an interesting empirical question. Some child care providers may envision their setting to be more akin to a primary group than a bureaucracy, with adult-child exchanges more closely approximating the parent-child relationship than a teacher-child relationship. For example, Honig (1989) argues that adult caregivers should not be detached from infants and toddlers.

Particular interest has been shown in discontinuities between families and early childhood programs involving children from low-income and ethnic minority families. The family-based socialization of children from cultural and linguistic minority families may differ significantly from the preparation schools assume children have had (Fillmore, 1988). Differences in value and language codes have been identified as major elements of home-school discontinuity here (Getzels, 1974). Consider the value code differences confronted by a child in a classroom that emphasizes the achievement ethic (i.e., delayed gratification, future success) but whose family experiences focus on basic survival (the present rather than the future, immediate rather than delayed gratification). The verbal environment of the preschool program also may differ markedly in interaction style, vocabulary, and syntactic structure in comparison with the child's family and neighborhood settings.

The effects of home-school discontinuity on children from low-income and ethnic minority families is pursued in the next section of this chapter. I turn now to research evidence on the extent to which these theoretically derived program-family discontinuities exist in reality.

The verbal environment of the preschool program also may differ markedly in interaction style, vocabulary, and syntactic structure in comparison with the child's family and neighborhood settings.

Socialization practices

Differences between mothers and teachers with regard to their goals, socialization pressures, control strategies, and interaction with young children have been found in a study by Robert Hess and his colleagues (Hess, Dickson, Price, & Leong, 1979; Hess, Price, Dickson, & Conroy, 1981). They gathered data through interviews, questionnaires, and observation of structured teaching interaction with children. The sample consisted of 34 teachers and 67 mothers and their first-born children. The mothers represented a range of socioeconomic backgrounds, and 14 were single parents at the time the study began. Fifteen of the teachers worked in full-day programs, 19 in half-day programs. All but four of the teachers had some type of certificate or credential in early childhood education.

While mothers and teachers were found to hold similar goals for children, mothers tended to emphasize social skills more than teachers did and to give less emphasis to independence. Mothers pressed for mastery of developmental tasks at an earlier age than did teachers. For instance, mothers as a group expected early socialization in social courtesy ("politeness"), while teachers thought this aspect of social development relatively less important for the child. On only one item ("Does not cry easily") did teachers expect earlier mastery than mothers. In a cluster of items dealing with emotional maturity, the item on which greatest difference appeared was "Can get over anger by himself." Few teachers expected mastery of anger before age 4, and about one-half did not see this as an important goal before age 6. Mothers expected children to be able to master anger at a much earlier age. These contrasts indicate difference between groups. There were large differences among individuals in both parent and teacher groups.

Hess and his colleagues found that mothers taught with a more direct, demanding, and explicit approach than did teachers. The investigators also found that mothers appealed to their own authority to obtain child compliance whereas teachers invoked rules more often. Further, teachers tended to be more flexible in implementing their requests for compliance.

Hess et al. (1981) suggest these behavior and attitude differences reflect larger patterns of childrearing and socialization that represent somewhat different views of the developmental capacities of young children. Mothers seem to believe that children are tougher and able to master skills at an early age. Teachers seem to view children as more tender, growing best when not pressured.

Parents do not see and relate to their young children the same way teachers do.

While it appears from these data that family and early childhood program offer somewhat different social environments for young children, a more refined analysis is needed to determine the level of discontinuity for individual children. The children involved in the teacher-child interactions in the Hess et al. study were not necessarily the children of parents in the study sample. Also, comparisons were made by group and not parent-teacher dyads.

The Hess et al. findings differ from the results of an earlier questionnaire study by Elardo and Caldwell (1973), who found that parents and teachers involved in an inner-city Little Rock, Arkansas, intervention program shared similar objectives and goals for children (e.g., to know concepts such as *smooth, round, scratchy;* to follow teachers' requests; to ask "Why" questions). Measurement strategies may account for the differences in the findings of these two investigations. Elardo and Caldwell asked respondents to rate the importance of each objective, whereas Hess et al. had respondents rank items through use of a paired-comparison technique. Ratings enable parents and teachers to consider all items as equally important whereas rankings force a decision about priorities.

Several observational studies have compared adult-child interaction in child care settings and in homes. Rubenstein and Howes (1979) examined social interaction and play behavior in a community-based child care center and at home for two matched groups of 18-month-old infants. The total sample size was 30. More adult-infant play, tactile contact, and reciprocal smiling were found in child care. More infant verbal responsiveness to maternal talking, more infant crying, and more maternal restrictiveness were found at home.

In a study of 36 children (mean age = 42 months), their mothers, and family day care providers, Long and Garduque (1987) found that children engaged in higher levels of instrumental help seeking (e.g., asked for material to maintain play) at home than in family day care. Caregivers and mothers differed in their responses to child initiations. Mothers displayed more social and facilitating responses to their children than did caregivers; they also were more likely to issue commands and suggest alternatives to the child's initiations. Caregivers responded more frequently than mothers with task-related compliments and used more positive reinforcement than mothers in initiating interactions with children. Compared to caregivers, mothers made more initiations that facilitated the child's entry into play or caregiving activity.

Teacher role may be a more significant influence on teachers' behavioral expectations than ethnic or social class background.

Ethnic and social class differences

Social class, ethnicity, and role (i.e., parent or teacher) have been found to be significantly related to differences between parents and teachers regarding behavioral expectations of preschool-aged children. Winetsky (1978) examined these variables in a study of 66 teachers and 172 parents associated with San Francisco area group-based preschool programs. Ethnic groups represented in the sample included Anglo-Americans, Latino-Americans, Black Americans, and Asian Americans, unevenly distributed between middle- and working-class categories. There were middle- and working-class groups of teachers since, until several years prior to the study, the state of California required only two years of college for licensure as a preschool "teacher." Using the Hollingshead Two-Factor Index of Social Position, Winetsky's study based social class of both teacher and parent groups on the social class position of their families.

Behavioral expectations were measured by the Educational Activities Index, a picture inventory that depicts consistent choices between the alternative value systems symbolically portrayed in a preschool situation. In each item (e.g., children engaging in a number activity) one picture of the pair represents a preschool situation where authority for decisions rests with the child (self-direction) and the other represents a situation in which authority for decisions rests with the teacher (conformity). The underlying values depicted in the drawings were based on the work of Melvin Kohn (1969), who found significant differences between middle- and working-class parents in the extent of preference for self-direction ("reliance upon internal standards") versus conformity ("compliance to externally imposed demands").

Winetsky found differences between the behavioral expectations of teachers in general and mothers who were either non-Anglo, working class, or both, but not between teachers and Anglo middle-class mothers. Middle-class parents expressed a higher degree of preference for self-direction than working-class parents. These differences remained significant when ethnicity was controlled. Teacher expectations, with a clear preference for self-direction, did not differ by social class and ethnicity. Winetsky indicates that the homogeneity of response of teachers suggests that their role acts to unify them in the behavioral expectations held for children. Teachers who were defined as working class by virtue of their husbands' occupations apparently were not significantly influenced by the values of their own family relationships and were similar to middle-class teachers in preferring self-direction. Assuming the preferred behaviors are borne out in actual home and school practices, these data indicate, then, that children whose families are neither middle class nor Anglo are likely to

Parental values contribute to child care decisions and indirectly to the level of continuity between family and child care setting.

___

experience discontinuity between home and school regardless of the ethnicity and social class of their preschool teacher.

The finding that teacher role may be a more significant influence on teachers' behavioral expectations than ethnic or social class background raises questions about a basis of recommendations for employing ethnic minority teachers to work with ethnic minority children. If teacher socialization processes involve the acquisition of new values and the loss of old ones for working-class and ethnic minority groups, then the training and hiring of more non-Anglo and working-class teachers may not yield the intended reduction of home-school discontinuity.

Discontinuity and parents' child care decisions

Parents' decisions about the type of care they use for their child may reduce the level of potential discontinuity between family and child care setting. It appears that parents are selective in their choice of child care arrangement. Phillips, Scarr, and McCartney (1987) found that parents who placed a high value on social skills and low value on conformity selected higher quality child care centers than did other parents. In a study by Clarke-Stewart (1987), parents who placed their children in a child care program or nursery school, versus a family day care home or no nonfamilial child care arrangement, wanted educational opportunities for their child. Similarly, parents of children in after-school child care programs have been found to rate the importance of children's educational experiences higher than parents of children in after-school self-care or family day care arrangements (Powell & Widdows, 1987). Hill-Scott (1987) also found parental conceptions of child care quality (i.e., physical facility vs. caregiver attributes) varied by type of program used by parents. In a Canadian study, parents using center-based child care indicated that the "program being offered" was an important influence on their selection of child care, while family day care users stressed "caregiver characteristics" in the selection of care (Pence & Goelman, 1987).

It appears, then, that parental values contribute to child care decisions and indirectly to the level of continuity between family and child care setting. Other family characteristics have been found to be associated with quality of child care arrangements. In a study of Los Angeles child care centers, Howes and Olenick (1986) found that working parents who had less stressful lives and were more competent and confident in their parenting were more likely to be associated with high-quality child care centers. Both teachers and parents of children in high-quality child care showed a willingness to negotiate compromise in interactions with children, whereas parents and teachers associated with low-quality centers exhibited

Children from low-resource families tend to participate in low-resource family day care homes.

---

a pattern of giving directions to children and expecting compliance (Howes, Goldenberg, Golub, Lee, & Olenick, 1984). Thus, these data suggest a relatively consistent pattern of socialization between home and child care environments. In Victoria, British Columbia, Goelman and Pence (1987a, 1987b) found that children of single mothers with low levels of education, occupation, and income tended to be disproportionately enrolled in low-quality family day care homes. These child care settings were generally rated as being of minimal quality in terms of the physical environment and the kinds of materials available to the children. Hence, children from low-resource families tended to participate in low-resource family day care homes.

Research data on the ways in which parents attempt to find child care also suggest that parents' child care choices may intentionally or unintentionally reduce the level of discontinuity between family and child care setting. In a study of urban parents' child care search behaviors (Powell & Eisenstadt, 1982), the general pattern was for parents to begin the search with nuclear family members and/or close friends and gradually move out to more peripheral ties such as acquaintances from work or other organizations. Formal sources such as newspapers, agencies, and telephone directories tended to be used toward the end of the search, and sometimes not at all. These findings suggest a tendency for parents to view child care as a private family matter. Peripheral ties were used when the inner circle of sources proved ineffective. Perhaps parents trusted their personal social networks to lead to quality child care that was compatible with their childrearing values and practices.

Summary

The existing evidence suggests that families and early childhood programs constitute different social environments for children in terms of childrearing values, behavioral expectations, and patterns of adult-child interaction. The data come from comparisons of mothers to adults in family day care settings, half-day nursery schools, and full-day child care centers. Differences between parents and teachers appear to be the most pronounced in instances where mothers are not Anglo and/or not middle class, regardless of the teacher's social class and ethnicity. With respect to child care, there is indirect evidence to suggest that parental decisions about child care arrangements may influence the level of home-school congruence. Such parent characteristics as values, parenting competence, and income have been found to be associated with the type and quality of care. While these matches may attenuate the level of discontinuity between

Parents begin the search for child care with nuclear family members and/or close friends and gradually move out to more peripheral ties such as acquaintances from work or other organizations.

family and child care setting, the result can also be children from low-resource families involved in minimal-quality or low-resource out-of-home care.

What are the effects of continuity and discontinuity on children?

Do children benefit if the family and child care settings are similar? Unfortunately, there is little research on this crucial question. Clarke-Stewart (1984, 1987) developed a measure of "mesh" between family and child care characteristics that included such variables as ethnic background, values, socioeconomic status, and age but found no significant correlations with child development. One possible reason for this lack of relationship is the limited range of family diversity: All families in this study were intact, and the majority were White and of middle- or professional-class status. Further, one quarter of the sample of mothers had worked or were working professionally with young children. There also may have been a limited range of quality in the child care programs: Clarke-Stewart (1987) presumes that, because of higher-than-average socioeconomic status, it is likely the families selected better-than-average child care.

Variations in the effects of discontinuity

It has been proposed that discontinuity between home and school is a major cause of the high frequency of scholastic failure among low-income and some ethnic minority populations. Much of the conceptual and empirical work along these lines has focused on culturally compatible education at the elementary and secondary level. The assumption of cultural compatibility is that education is more effective if children are taught in a context and through a process that is consistent with their natal culture (Tharp, 1989). Attention has been given primarily to the processes of teaching and learning in Black, Hispanic, and Native-American cultures because children from these groups generally have difficulty in schools organized by and for the dominant culture. Student performance has been found to improve when school processes are changed to be more compatible with the students' culture. A major research and demonstration project in this area is the Kamehameha Early Education Program (KEEP), which has developed and examined a culturally compatible language arts program for kindergarten through third grade children of Hawaiian ancestry (Tharp et al., 1984). Hawaiian children in standard schools are among the lower achieving minorities in the United States, but in KEEP classrooms

Probably the extent to which the family and the school share a common system for teaching and learning depends in part on the length of the parents' schooling experience.

Student performance has been found to improve when school processes are changed to be more compatible with the students' culture.

An appropriate level of discontinuity between family and child care settings may help children adjust to social demands in the diverse situations they encounter as they move out of the home.

they have been found to approach national norms on standard achievement tests (Tharp, 1982; Tharp & Gallimore, 1988).

Laosa (1982) has pointed to the level of parental schooling as a major influence on a child's adaptation to the demands of a standard classroom. He hypothesizes that children of more highly schooled parents learn to master in their homes the form and dynamics of teaching and learning processes that are similar to those of the school classroom. Because these children learn to master classroomlike interaction processes in their homes, they have a decided advantage over children of lower schooling parents who provide their children with teaching and learning processes that have comparatively little adaptive value in the classroom. Laosa's model posits that the extent to which the family and the school share a common system for teaching and learning depends in part on the length of the parents' schooling experience. In a study of Chicano and non-Hispanic White mothers, he found that ethnic group differences in maternal teaching strategies became statistically nonsignificant when length of maternal schooling was controlled (Laosa, 1980). The basis of Laosa's model is his findings from a series of studies that suggest (a) a relationship between mothers' teaching style and children's characteristic approaches to learning, (b) a relationship between length of maternal schooling and maternal teaching style, and (c) a resemblance between the teaching strategies of the more highly schooled mothers and the instructional strategies of academic classrooms.

Teacher and parent attitudes stemming from social class and racial stereotypes also may contribute to low academic performance. Some teachers may maintain low achievement expectations of children from particular ethnic and socioeconomic groups; further, some low-income and ethnic minority parents may hold negative perceptions of schools in general and teachers in particular. Presumably home-school relationships under these conditions are far from optimal for the child (Lightfoot, 1978).

An appropriate level of discontinuity between family and child care settings may be beneficial to the child. It may help children adjust to social demands in the diverse situations they encounter as they move out of the home into the wider social world (Long & Garduque, 1987). The mothers and caregivers interviewed in the Long and Garduque (1987) study suggested that family day care provided children with opportunities to be with peers and extended family members, and to learn rules and values that might differ from the ones encountered in their own homes. The experience was seen as helpful to children in learning to cope with different environments.

Ethnocentrism is conveyed to parents and children when school practices are defined in the narrow, traditional terms of the dominant culture.

These ideas are reminiscent of the observation of sociologist Willard Waller more than a half century ago. Waller (1932) suggested that "the child develops better if he is treated impersonally in the schools, provided the parents are there to supply the needed personal attitudes" (p. 69). He maintained it would be a "sad day" if parent-teacher relations succeeded in "getting parents to see children more or less as teachers see them."

Bronfenbrenner (1979) has argued theoretically that participation in more than one setting has positive developmental effects when the settings occur in culturally diverse environments (i.e., vary by social class, ethnicity, religion, and other background characteristics). He assumes that the developing person's adaptation to a variety of people, tasks, and situations in a range of settings increases the scope and flexibility of the individual's cognitive competence and social skills.

Melson (in press) has speculated that exposure to different socialization agents who present distinctive sets of behaviors and expectations may enhance a child's ideas about the various individuals who have influence over aspects of the child's life. For example, the preschool-age child who is cared for at home, at a child care center, and by a regular sitter may develop a more differentiated set of expectations concerning who "takes care" of him or her, where, at what times, and in what ways than the child who is solely home-reared.

The distinction between *creative conflict* and *negative dissonance* has been offered by Lightfoot (1978) in her analysis of relations between families and schools. The former represents differences between family and school that are inevitable in a complex society and help children become more malleable and responsive to a changing world. Absolute homogeneity between family and school would reflect a static, authoritarian society and discourage creative, adaptive development in children. Lightfoot suggests that negative dissonance occurs when differences between schools and families accentuate and reinforce power and status inequities in society. The message of ethnocentrism is conveyed to parents and children when school practices are defined in the narrow, traditional terms of the dominant culture. According to Lightfoot, creative conflict exists when there is a balance of power and responsibilities between family and school, not when the family's role is negated or diminished.

Lippitt (1968) has proposed five patterns of problem solving children adopt in response to differences in expectations, pressures, and needs from parents, teachers, peers, and the self. One strategy is *compartmentalized loyalty,* whereby the child denies the issue of conflict by keeping relationships in separate compartments (e.g., when in the presence of a teacher, a parent has no psychological existence). Another way to resolve these

Understanding the conditions under which discontinuity is beneficial or harmful to children remains a major research task.

---

complexities is to make one of the sources psychologically dominant, treating the other source(s) as irrelevant, incorrect, or misleading. Lippitt refers to this pattern as *pervasive dominant loyalty.* A third solution involves *rejecting the references* by in effect saying, "If you can't agree, then there are no authoritative standards, and I am free to do what seems most attractive to me" (p. 347). As a fourth option, children may opt for *striking a balance* by attempting to arrive at some kind of compromise that will please all parties involved. Lippitt indicates this strategy may result in dissatisfaction and discontent and is likely to have little positive contribution to the development of self-identity. In the fifth pattern, *integration and reciprocal influence,* the child has learned that his decisions and actions "belong to him." He is not simply a target of pressure from others but has a reciprocal relationship with others.

Understanding the conditions under which discontinuity is beneficial or harmful to children remains a major research task. In particular, research needs to take the child's perspective on discontinuity (Melson, in press). Are children aware of the similarities and differences of various socialization agents in their lives? Are children's adjustments to different settings influenced by their understanding of differences among socialization agents?

Potential mediating variables

At a theoretical level, it appears that discontinuity offers the child both developmental opportunities and risks. Peters and Kontos (1987) have proposed that the probable impact of discontinuity depends on: (1) the *magnitude* of the discrepancy (greater levels of discontinuity constitute a greater threat); (2) the *duration* of the discrepancy; (3) the *timing* of the events in the sense of sensitive periods of development as well as being "on time" or "off time" as a normative transition; and (4) the *preparation* for and understanding of changes and discrepancies, including *communication* about the transition.

The aforementioned concerns of Laosa and Lightfoot regarding ethnic and status differences are illustrative of the *magnitude* factor. The *timing* factor is perhaps at the crux of long-standing debates in this country about the use of full-time nonfamilial care for children under 5 years of age. The transition to school creates discontinuity for children, but because it is a normative "on time" developmental transition in our society there is no widespread concern about its appropriateness (Long & Garduque, 1987). Growth in the use of nonfamilial child care may contribute to societal conceptions of child care as an "on time" transition, but considerable research is needed to resolve questions as to whether the nonfamilial care of

The transition to school creates discontinuity for children, but because it is a normative "on time" developmental transition in our society there is no widespread concern about its appropriateness.

The child's contribution to the experience of discontinuity has received limited attention in the literature but certainly must be recognized as a potentially significant influence.

infants is "off time" in the sense of a sensitive period of development (Belsky, 1988). Children's previous experiences illustrate the *preparation* factor. For instance, the child care setting may have elements in common with being cared for by a sitter, and older children may come to the situation with expectations based on television shows or reports of older siblings or peers (Hood & McHale, 1987).

The child's contribution to the experience of discontinuity has received limited attention in the literature but certainly must be recognized as a potentially significant influence. Rubenstein and Howes (1979) found that differences between home and center in adult-child interaction were often a function of differences in infant as well as adult behavior. Children might experience consistency in their social environment because their physical or behavioral characteristics may evoke similar responses from different people, or because their roles and relationships may be similar across settings. For instance, the oldest child in a family may be given the extra responsibility of helping care for young siblings and assume a similar role in a family day care home in relation to younger children (Hood & McHale, 1987). Child attributes such as temperament, flexibility, and social competence also are likely to influence adjustment to diverse settings. Some children may be more adaptable than others in moving from one attachment figure and setting to another (Gewirtz, 1978).

Children's responses to discontinuity between home and early childhood setting also may be influenced by the level of consistency *within* a particular setting. Inconsistency could be a function of a sole adult (e.g., family day care provider) functioning in an inconsistent manner with a child; two or more adults in the same setting (e.g., parents, see Palkovitz, 1987) behaving in distinctly different ways; or instability in the adult composition of a setting, such as staff turnover in a child care center (Cummings, 1980).

Summary

Little is known about the effects on children of continuity and discontinuity between families and early childhood settings. It has been proposed that home-school discontinuity contributes to the generally low academic achievement of ethnic minority children and children of parents with relatively few years of education. This is an area of crucial importance in need of further investigation. For children who are being reared in the dominant culture and/or whose parents are educated, there are theoretical arguments from a number of scholars that appropriate levels and types of between-system differences may positively influence a child's cognitive competence and adaptive behaviors. Future research needs to transcend global and dichotomous treatments of the continuity construct to identify the factors that contribute to positive and negative child effects of continuity and discontinuity between families and early childhood settings.

What is the effect on children of efforts to strengthen connections between family and early childhood program?

Leaders in the early childhood field have long argued that children are "the real winners" in collaborative ties between teachers and parents (Hymes, 1953, p. 9). Is there an empirical foundation of such claims? This section examines theory and research on the question: What is the effect on children of efforts to strengthen connections between family and early childhood program?

Theoretical perspectives

In the past several decades there has been growing theoretical interest among social scientists in the potential negative effects on the child of participation in multiple socialization agencies (e.g., home, school, community groups) that do not maintain supportive linkages. For example, in an analysis of trends in modern social authority over children, Smelser (1965) suggested a key problem is the possible discontinuity between various authorities that are imposed on children. As society becomes more heterogeneous, complex, and mobile, a critical social problem is that of relations between parents and other authority figures. Lippitt (1968) proposed that much of the efficacy of socialization involving two or more socialization agencies "depends on the type of communication and coordination that takes place between agents and agencies" (p. 344).

More recently, Bronfenbrenner (1979) generated a number of hypotheses and assumptions about the conditions that enhance the development of individuals who function in multiple settings. He refers to the set of interrelations between two or more settings in which an individual is a participant as the *mesosystem*. His interest in this system is embedded within his larger theoretical treatment of human development from an ecological perspective.

Specifically, Bronfenbrenner hypothesized that a setting's developmental potential is enhanced when:

- the role demands in the different settings are compatible, and there is goal consensus between settings.
- there are supportive linkages between settings, especially when the developing person's experience and sense of competence in the new setting is limited or nonexistent (as in the case of children, or of minorities entering a majority milieu). The least favorable condition for development is where between-setting links are nonsupportive or completely absent.
- an individual's entry into a new setting is made in the company of one or more persons with whom she or he has participated in other settings (e.g., a parent accompanies child to the preschool).
- there is open two-way communication between settings that includes the family in the communications network.
- the mode of communication between settings is personal (face-to-face versus printed announcement).

Using home-school relations as an example, Bronfenbrenner proposed that development would be advanced for children participating in home and school environments where interconnections are

> characterized by more frequent interactions between parents and school personnel, a greater number of persons known in common by members of the two settings, and more frequent communications between home and school, more information in each setting about the other, but always with the proviso that such interconnections not undermine the motivation and capacity of those persons who deal directly with the child to act in his behalf. This qualification gives negative weight to actions by school personnel that degrade parents or to parental demands that undermine the professional morale or effectiveness of the teacher. (Bronfenbrenner, 1979, p. 218)

Are there research data to support these theoretical propositions? To answer this question, different strategies of fostering home-program connections need to be considered. The studies reviewed here are organized by two different approaches: parents as facilitators of their child's entry into the early childhood program and parents as learners of child development and parenting information through a formal parent education component of the early childhood program.

Certainly these linkage modes are not the only ways to establish and maintain connections between family and early childhood program. Unfortunately, little research has been done regarding the effects on children of other methods of linking home and school (see the summary at end of this chapter).

*Toddlers show distress behaviors during the parents'
departures more frequently than infants and preschool-age
children.*

Parents as facilitators of child's preschool entry

Several studies provide useful empirical data on the effects of parents' efforts to ease a child's entry into an early childhood program. Schwarz and Wynn (1971) conducted one of the first and few investigations of children's responses to maternal involvement in facilitating preschool entry. They studied 108 middle-class 4-year-old children enrolled in a laboratory nursery school. The experimental comparison involved (a) a visit by child and mother to the classroom prior to the start of classes versus no visit and (b) the mother's presence in the classroom for 20 minutes of the class session versus the mother's immediate departure. The results indicated that neither a visit to the nursery school nor the mother's presence in the classroom for part of the first session facilitated the child's emotional adjustment to the nursery school. A large majority of the children exhibited a rapid and uneventful adaptation to the preschool setting. Ratings on several indexes of emotional reactions were made the first day of class and one and five weeks later.

The strategies employed in the Schwarz and Wynn experiment may have yielded different results with children younger than 4 years. A study of the leave-takings and reunions of 56 middle-class children in a full-day university nursery school found that toddlers showed distress behaviors during the parents' departures more frequently than infants and preschool-age children (Field et al., 1984). Toddlers exhibited more hovering, attention getting, verbal protest, clinging, and crying; their parents showed more hovering, distracting behaviors, and sneaking out of the classroom. Also, in this study infants and toddlers related primarily to their parents upon arrival at their classroom, whereas preschool-age children related to their teachers.

Parents' provision of information to children about an impending transition to a new setting, a strategy not examined in the Schwarz and Wynn experiment, is related to children's reactions to the separation. In a study conducted in an experimental playroom, Weinraub and Lewis (1977) found that the distress exhibited by 2-year-olds upon the mother's departure was related to the mother's verbal explanation of the leave-taking. The children of mothers who slipped out of the room without saying anything were least likely to play and most likely to cry. Mothers who informed their children they were leaving and/or would return shortly and also gave their children instructions as to what to do in their absence had children who were most likely to play and least likely to cry. In a subsequent experiment, Weinraub (1977) found that boys exhibited less

Mothers who inform their children that they are leaving and/or will return shortly and also give their children instructions as to what to do in their absence have children who are most likely to play and least likely to cry.

distress when mothers explained their leave-taking than when mothers left without saying anything. The Field et al. (1984) investigation yielded a similar finding for both boys and girls: Parents' verbal explanations accounted for the largest amount of variance in child verbal protest.

Research findings also suggest that parent attributes and behaviors may contribute to children's reactions to leave-taking. In the Field et al. (1984) study, children dropped off by the mother as opposed to the father showed more frequent attention-getting and crying behaviors, and mothers showed more frequent distracting-the-child tactics and took longer to leave the classroom than did fathers. These variables accounted for a significant amount of the variance in crying behavior. Interestingly, another study found that 40% of the mothers but none of the fathers worried about their infants' impending responses to departures (Weinraub & Frankel, 1977).

Parents as learners

A considerable amount of research has been conducted on the effects of parent education programs for families with young children. Unlike the investigations reviewed above, the bulk of these researches has involved low-income parents of children enrolled in an early intervention program. Generally the intent of the program's parent education component is to help parents carry out parent-child activities and communicate attitudes at home that extend and reinforce the work of the preschool intervention — in other words, to maximize continuity between home and school.

While recent reviews of the parent education and support literature point to some positive program effects on children (see Chapter 4), most of the studies do not directly assess the relative impact of a parent education component in a program that includes direct work with the child *and* with the parent(s). The question here is whether the effects of an early childhood program are strengthened and/or sustained for a longer period of time when there is a systematic focus on the parent and the child compared to a focus on the child only. Most of the existing studies cannot answer this question because (a) the intervention viewed the parent as the primary teacher and therefore did not include separate work with the preschool child (e.g., a parent-focused home visitation program that does not involve direct work with the child independent of the parent), or (b) the evaluation design and/or data analyses did not consider the separate effects of treatment conditions involving preschool only versus preschool plus parent participation. In an extensive review of the early (1960s and early 1970s) literature on the effects of early intervention, Bronfenbrenner (1974) concluded that "the involvement of the child's family as an active participant is critical to the success to any intervention program" (p. 55). This conclusion is based largely on findings of several studies of the independent contribution of parent involvement to preschool effects. The investigations found that program work with parents did not contribute substantially to initial IQ gains beyond the gains attributed to a preschool program, but that parent participation in the intervention helped to sustain IQ gains after the program ended.

Findings of a well-designed study by Radin, which contributed to Bronfenbrenner's conclusion, warrant attention here. Radin (1972) investigated the effects of three degrees of maternal involvement in a compensatory preschool program enrolling 4-year-old children from low-income families. Seventy-one children were divided into three matched treatment groups. Children in each group were offered a half-day nursery school four days a week. In addition, Group A children received a biweekly home tutorial session involving the mothers, and mothers were invited to participate in a weekly small group meeting focused on childrearing practices. Group B children also received the home tutorial session involving the mother but mothers were not invited to attend the weekly group meetings. Group C children received a tutorial session without the mother and their mothers were not invited to participate in the weekly group meetings. Children were administered vocabulary and intelligence tests and were rated on classroom behavior; mothers were assessed in regard to childrearing attitudes and cognitive aspects of the home environment.

Radin found no differences in the children at the end of the one-year program in terms of intellectual growth and classroom behavior. However, mothers who were offered the opportunity for maximum participation (Group A) exhibited the most change in attitudes toward authoritarianism and provision of educational materials in the home. Mothers who received the least level of involvement (Group C) showed no change in the areas measured. In a follow-up assessment of one-third of the children at the end of kindergarten, Radin discovered significant differences between the groups with (Groups A and B) and without (Group C) maternal involvement in subsequent IQ scores and gains in IQ scores. Further, the group with no maternal involvement (Group C) showed no continuation of verbal growth during the kindergarten year. Given the small sample size of the follow-up study (n = 24), the results need to be treated as suggestive.

Research on the effects of parent participation in Head Start provides little information on the question at hand. In spite of the major emphasis on families in descriptions of Head Start goals (e.g., O'Keefe, 1979), few good studies have examined Head Start's impact on families. The most widespread parent training programs regularly conducted in local Head Start programs ("Exploring Parenting" and "Getting Involved") have not been systematically evaluated in terms of their impact on children and their families (McKey et al., 1985). However, some investigators have examined special interventions added to Head Start to train parents to be their children's educators. In a review of studies of these parent-focused interventions, the Head Start Synthesis Project (McKey et al., 1985) concluded it was unclear whether special programs that help parents teach their children academic skills have an effect on either parents or children. Some studies reported significant gains by children whose parents received special parent-as-educator training, while other studies showed no impact.

The Head Start Synthesis Project was able to identify only 5 studies that satisfied the criteria for inclusion in a meta-analysis used to produce a numerical estimate of effects. The meta-analysis focused on the relatively narrow question of "What is the effect of high parent involvement in Head Start compared to low parent involvement on child cognitive measures?"

The results indicated that children whose parents were highly involved in Head Start performed better than children whose parents were less involved. Program involvement generally entailed participation in a parent education component such as home visitation. This finding is of limited use, however. As McKey et al. point out, there are no assurances that the low- and high-involvement parents (and their children) were equivalent at the outset of the program. Parents themselves controlled their level of involvement, and hence such factors as parental motivation and interest in their child's performance may have influenced both parent involvement and child achievement.

Debate about the effects of parent participation in early intervention with disabled preschoolers has intensified in recent years largely due to the report of a meta-analysis of primary research studies investigating the efficacy of early intervention. Analyzing 74 studies, Casto and Mastropieri (1986) concluded that parents can be effective interveners but "they are probably not essential to intervention success, and those intervention programs which utilize parents are not more effective than those which do not" (p. 421). Some scholars interested in early childhood education have cited the Casto and Mastropieri finding to support the position that parent-focused interventions are no more effective than child-focused interventions (e.g., Clarke-Stewart, 1988).

The Casto and Mastropieri results cannot be used to address the question of whether early childhood programs that involve parents are more effective than those that do not. Contrary to the impression created by the Casto and Mastropieri (1986) statement that "those intervention programs which utilize parents are not more effective than those which do not" (p. 421), the analysis did not compare treatment conditions involving children only versus children plus their parents. For each study included in the meta-analysis, the investigators coded the degree of parent involvement into one of four categories: (1) "only intervenor" (parent delivers intervention and receives supervision but no one else works with child); (2) "major intervenor" (parent is responsible for intervention activities 25% or more of the time); (3) "minor intervenor" (parent is responsible for intervention activities 10 to 25% of time); and (4) "not involved in intervention" (parent involved in less than 10% of time in actual intervention activities). The analysis compared categories 1 and 2 versus categories 3 and 4, thereby confounding degree of program focus on parent and child. Apparently, programs serving children only were combined with programs where parents were involved less than 10% of the time (fourth category). Hence, this category's title "not involved in intervention" is inaccurate (Strain & Smith, 1986). Unlike the aforementioned

Several evaluations of parent education initiatives of elementary schools have found positive effects on children's academic performance.

Bronfenbrenner review, the Casto and Mastropieri meta-analysis did not consider a three-way comparison of treatment conditions involving child only versus parent only versus child plus parent; programs aimed at parents (first category) were combined with a set of programs aimed at both child and parent (second category).

Several evaluations of parent education initiatives of elementary schools have found positive effects on children's academic performance (see Henderson [1987] for an annotated bibliography of research showing positive impact). One of the most extensive and ambitious interventions into home-school relations is reported by Mildred Smith (1968). A program designed to improve school performance of low-income minority children in Flint, Michigan, elementary grades employed a number of procedures to provide information and social support to parents regarding their educator role. For instance, parents were encouraged to provide their child with a quiet space for homework and to engage their child in reading, and they were provided with such supports as a child's dictionary for the home and information meetings on school activities. As Bronfenbrenner (1979) has observed, the experiment involved nearly all of the interconnections he has stipulated theoretically as important for enhancing development in two settings.

The 1,000 children and their parents involved in the Flint program at two elementary schools were compared to a population in two other Flint public elementary schools serving families of similar socioeconomic backgrounds. Unfortunately, a limited range of potential outcomes was assessed. The results showed significant gains in reading achievement and positive parental reactions to the program.

In a longitudinal study of 293 third and fifth grade children from 14 classrooms where teachers varied significantly in their emphasis on parent involvement, Epstein (in press) found that teacher leadership in parent involvement in home learning activities significantly influenced positive change in reading achievement. There was no significant relationship between parent involvement practices and math achievement, however. In an experiment by Tizard, Schofield, and Hewison (1982), 1,900 elementary school students in working-class London neighborhoods were assigned to three treatment conditions: In one treatment, parents received support from the school for helping their child read at home; in a second group, children received extra reading help twice weekly at school from a teacher; and a control group received no special reading assistance beyond the routine school instruction. Children who practiced reading at home with their parents showed significant gains in reading achievement in comparison with the control group and the children who received special assistance from teachers at school.

This review of the effects on children of efforts to strengthen connections between family and early childhood program is informative in terms of what it does not include.

Summary

Research on the effects of two different modes of strengthening connections between family and early childhood setting was reviewed in this section. With regard to parents' roles in facilitating their child's entry into an early childhood program, there is evidence to support the practice of parents verbally preparing the child for the leave-taking at the early childhood program. In several studies, parents' explanations of their departures were associated with reduced levels of distress exhibited by the child. Existing research does not provide a justification for several other practices surrounding parents' facilitation of their child's school entry, however. A well-designed study involving middle-class 4-year-olds failed to provide empirical support for the practice of mother and child visits to the nursery school prior to entering the program and for the practice of mothers remaining with their child for part of the first session at nursery school. It is not known how younger children (especially toddlers), children of ethnic minority and low-income backgrounds, and children entering full-day child care for the first time would have responded to this experiment.

With regard to home-school relations strategies that emphasize parent education, the studies reviewed here involving children younger than 6 years provide no evidence that a systematic focus on both the parent and the child significantly strengthens immediate gains in the child's cognitive competence when compared to a child-focused preschool. However, several studies involving elementary school children show significant gains in reading performance among children of parents involved in a special educational program offered by the school. There is suggestive but inconclusive evidence from research on early intervention programs to indicate that when the program includes a parent education component, children's cognitive gains from a preschool experience are sustained for a longer period of time after the program ends; cognitive gains erode more rapidly after program termination when parents are not involved in the program.

This review of the effects on children of efforts to strengthen connections between family and early childhood program is informative in terms of what it does not include. There is an impressive dearth of research on this topic. Moreover, most of the studies have considered a narrow set of child outcomes (e.g., IQ) and have been conducted within a program context (early intervention program serving children from low-income families) that seriously limits generalizations to other situations (e.g., child care programs).

Most of the hypotheses presented earlier in this chapter (i.e., Bronfenbrenner's propositions) have not been tested. There is virtually no empirical understanding of the assumed causal pathway that parent-teacher collaboration leads to improved home-school continuity that in turn leads to improved child competence. What are the consequences for children of varying types and frequencies of communication between parents and caregivers? What are the effects on children of parents assuming different program roles such as participation in policy decisions? The effects on children of parent participation in multiple program roles also is not clear, although it is possible that long-term participation in many program roles (e.g., classroom volunteer, member of governance body, participant in parent education activities) may have more impact than concentrated participation in one or two roles.

General summary and conclusions

This chapter has examined theory and research regarding the continuity of children's experiences between families and early childhood programs. Linkage (e.g., communication) and congruence (e.g., similar childrearing goals) dimensions of continuity have been emphasized in addressing three major questions: To what extent do discontinuities exist between families and early childhood programs? What are the effects of continuity/discontinuity on children? What is the effect on children of efforts to strengthen connections between families and early childhood programs? This final section of the chapter summarizes the existing knowledge and suggests where might the field go from here.

The theoretical argument for collaborative connections between families and early childhood programs is quite robust. In brief, the theoretical work reviewed in this chapter suggests that discontinuities between family and early childhood program are inevitable and probably of greatest magnitude for children from low-income and ethnic minority families; that appropriate levels and types of discontinuity (largely unspecified) enhance a child's cognitive competence and adaptive skills, but major between-system discontinuities can lead to maladaptive behavior and poor academic performance; and that supportive linkages between socialization agencies contribute to a child's ease of adjustment to a new early childhood setting and to overall (largely unspecified) child competence.

What we know and do not know from research may be summarized as follows:

1. There are discontinuities between families and nonfamilial socialization agencies in the form of differences between parents and teachers in values, expectations of child behavior, and styles of adult-child interaction. The differences appear to be greatest for children whose parents are non-Anglo and not middle class.

2. We do not know the effects on children of discontinuities between families and early childhood programs, although it can be inferred from existing research that home-school differences are likely to constitute an educational risk for children whose parents have limited formal education and/or are of some ethnic minority backgrounds (especially Black, Hispanic, and Native American).

3. The efficacy of most practices aimed at strengthening linkages between families and early childhood programs is unknown. For children under 6 years of age, there is evidence to suggest that children benefit from mothers providing verbal explanations to the child of leave-taking at an early childhood program. There is inconclusive evidence that children benefit from frequent participation in parent education activities coordinated with the preschool program content. This latter practice in elementary schools has been found to have a positive effect on children's reading competence, however. Two other recommended practices — a mother and child visit to the early childhood program and mother remaining with the child during the initial school session — have been found to have no positive effect on the emotional adjustment of 4-year-old middle-class children to a half-day nursery school. Because several generations of early childhood educators have advocated these practices, it would be important for further and more comprehensive research to be carried out before conclusions are reached about the value of previsits and parental presence during a child's initial entry into a new setting. The effects of other practices have not been studied systematically, and the existing studies have considered a limited number of child outcome areas and types of programs.

Inappropriate generalization of research data has been a problem in the early childhood education field (Clarke-Stewart & Fein, 1983), and the above findings are not exempt from misuse. In addition to being sparse, these data are limited in their applicability to diverse program settings and population groups. The findings regarding the positive effects of a parent education component are illustrative here. The research yielding positive effects (e.g., Radin, 1972) dealt with long-term early intervention programs serving low-income families. The parent education components were intensive, involving frequent (usually weekly) home visits and/or parent group meetings. The content was directly connected to preschool program activities in an effort to strengthen home-school continuity. Data generated in this context cannot be generalized to the modal situation where a half-day nursery school or full-day child care center serving working- and middle-class parents offers periodic (monthly or less often) parent education sessions, the content of which is likely to vary from session to session and may or may not be directly linked to the preschool curriculum.

The existing research findings justify recommendations for strengthening relations between families and early childhood programs that serve ethnic minority children and/or children whose parents have limited education. Data suggest this population is likely to experience discontinuities between home and early childhood program that may adversely affect the development of social and academic competence. Existing research findings offer limited guidance on what types of changes in the home-school relationship would have a positive impact on children from ethnic minority and low-income families, however. For programs serving Anglo children from middle-class families, there is an insufficient data base for assessing the merits of arguments for strengthening connections between family and early childhood program. Many key assumptions of home-school linkage practices have not been subjected to rigorous investigation, and studies of the effects of some practices have yielded inconclusive results.

From the literature reviewed in this chapter, it is reasonable to conclude that *from a child development perspective, the theoretical grounds are significantly stronger than the empirical foundation of rationales for establishing and maintaining cooperative relations between families and early childhood programs.*

What are the implications of this conclusion for the field of early childhood education? The combination of existing theoretical work and research data provides a strong argument for significantly increasing the level of field-based experimentation with strategies for strengthening relations between families and early childhood programs. A general conceptual guide for research exists; there are theoretically driven hypotheses that need and deserve to be examined. Experienced practitioners have an important role to play here by helping to generate, refine, and test specific practices. Given the limited research base, the field needs to assume a critical and analytic stance toward assumptions and practices that long have been a dominant force in the field but have yet to be systematically examined.

Chapter 3

From the perspective of adults: Relations between parents and early childhood programs

I N THIS CHAPTER we change the lens through which we view relations between families and early childhood programs. In contrast with the child focus of Chapter 2, the present chapter considers adult views of the processes by which families and early childhood practitioners share the task of socializing and educating young children. The aim is to review what is known about adults' experiences in managing relations between families and early childhood programs. The chapter draws upon research involving half-day nursery schools, full-day child care centers, Head Start, and family day care programs to examine the nature, predictors, and effects on parents of parent-staff relationships.

The chapter consists of two major sections. The first and largest section reviews research findings regarding the characteristics and correlates of relations between parents and early childhood personnel. The second section summarizes the literature on effects of parent participation in early childhood programs.

A prefatory comment is in order about the use of the term *parent* in the chapter's title and text. Generally this label refers to mothers. Data indicate that it is primarily mothers who search for child care (Powell & Eisenstadt, 1982) and maintain contact with early childhood program staff (Powell, 1978b; Zigler & Turner, 1982). Use of the term *parent* in this chapter is in acknowledgment of the handful of fathers who carry out tasks traditional American gender roles have assigned to women.

Dimensions of the parent-staff relationship

This section begins with a brief description and analysis of prevailing sociological views of family-school relations. The applicability of existing theoretical frameworks to early childhood programs is noted. The bulk of the section pertains to the following dimensions of the parent-staff relationship: profiles of parent participation in child care and Head Start programs; mode, content, and frequency of parent-staff communication; uses and potential misuses of information exchanged between parents and staff; perceptions of parenting abilities; the role of parent-child and caregiver-child separation and attachment feelings; and parent and staff preferences for the parent-staff relationship. The section concludes with a review of research on predictors of differences in relations between parents and early childhood staff.

For the most part, this monograph deals with existing relations between families and early childhood programs. As described in Chapter 2, the process through which connections are made between parents and early childhood programs appears to involve explicit or implicit selection criteria that result in family-program matches of similar quality. This monograph does not deal with parental preferences for child care arrangements, but interested readers are referred to a growing body of research literature on this subject (Bradbard, Endsley, & Readdick, 1983; Endsley, Bradbard, & Readdick, 1984; Bogat & Gensheimer, 1986; Fuqua & Labensohn, 1986; Atkinson, 1987).

The theory of optimal social distance

Proponents of an open, two-way flow of information and influence between family and early childhood program generally hasten to add a qualifier that underscores the need to respect the boundaries and special contributions of family and school. Such qualifiers typically acknowledge the desire of many teachers to limit parental tampering with their professional judgments, and the wish of parents to avoid professional intrusion into family affairs.

These views are consonant with sociology's dominant theoretical treatment of relations between families and schools. Sociological analyses emphasize the distinctive roles of parents and teachers within their respective settings, and the unique properties and functions of family and nonfamilial childrearing settings. This perspective gives rise to a largely organizational question: What level and type of interaction between parents and childrearing professionals is in the best interest of the family as well as the early childhood program? That is, what type of home-school relationship maintains the characteristic goals and functions of each setting?

The prevailing response to this question from sociologists is that optimal social distance between home and school protects each setting's distinctive characteristics (Litwak & Meyer, 1974). Conflicts between parents and teachers are viewed as an inevitable and natural result of differences in the scope and function of families and schools. Willard Waller, whose classic book on teaching offered one of the earliest sociologi-

What type of participation exists when centers encourage or do not encourage parental presence at the center?

---

cal analyses of parent-teacher relations, depicted parents and teachers as living "in a condition of mutual distrust and enmity" (Waller, 1932, p. 68). He devoted the bulk of his book's chapter on parents and teachers to suggestions on how school officials should handle complaints from parents (e.g., "meet disgruntled patrons with a poised and friendly air that effectively discourages their definition of the situation as a personal quarrel," p. 74). More recently, Lightfoot (1978) suggested that discontinuities between families and schools largely are a function of their structural properties and their cultural histories and purposes.

Balance theory is a major paradigm within this approach to home-school relations. This framework, set forth by Litwak and Meyer (1974) in regard to elementary and secondary schools, calls for "optimal social distance . . . between the extremes of intimacy and isolation" (p. 6). It is in contrast with a "closed door" position where community participation is kept to a minimum because the presence of parents would hamper staff in the performance of their duties. It also is in contrast with an "open door" position, which assumes that many basic educational processes take place in the family, peer group, and neighborhood, thus necessitating close school-community contacts.

A key premise of balance theory is that basic educational processes require experts to handle uniform tasks and nonexperts to handle nonuniform tasks. Nonuniform tasks involve situations where the knowledge of ordinary citizens is as great as that of experts, or where there is no expert knowledge. Litwak and Meyer propose that educational processes would be impaired if experts dominated all uniform and nonuniform tasks, or if nonexperts tried to handle all uniform tasks (i.e., because parents lack professional training and have strong emotional ties to their child, they would inhibit the use of professional judgment). Hence, according to balance theory, communication between schools and families should not bring them into such close contact that "they impair the social structures that are required to sustain each" (p. 13).

For the early childhood field, a limitation of balance theory and similar perspectives is that the scope of functions of most early childhood settings is not narrowly circumscribed. The younger the child, the wider the range of functioning for which adults must assume responsibility (Katz, 1980). Thus, it is unusual for an early childhood setting to see its mission as primarily or totally instructional, leaving noninstructional functions to the family. This state of affairs leads to two related consequences of significance to the study of parent-staff relations: (1) the work of early childhood practitioners is likely to be viewed as similar to the tasks of parenting and, as a result, (2) territoriality issues stemming from unclear role boundaries are likely to be problematic.

There is a wide range in the extent to which parents in any one center participate.

Profiles of participation

Unfortunately, there is not a recent national profile of the ways in which parents participate in early childhood programs, and existing statistical descriptions are limited in scope and detail. There is information, albeit dated, on the level of parent participation in child care centers and Head Start programs.

Full-day child care. The supply study component of the National Day Care Study is the largest survey ever undertaken of center-based child care in the United States (Coelen, Glantz, & Calore, 1979). Conducted in 1976–1977, the study included approximately one out of six child care centers in each of the 50 states plus the District of Columbia. Data were collected primarily by telephone interviews with staff at 3,167 child care centers.

Counseling on child development was provided by 86% of the centers in this national probability sample. Fifty-five percent provided family counseling, 45% offered assistance in obtaining food stamps or financial aid, and 52% provided assistance in obtaining community services. Only about 33% of the centers provided all four of these services to parents, and 10% provided none.

The supply study also collected information on five modes of parent participation. Thirty-five percent of the centers nationally indicated that parents were involved in reviewing center budgets and programs. Parent participation in staff selection reportedly occurred at 22% of the centers, and 28% reported that parents served as center volunteers. Thirty-five percent of the centers indicated that parents used the center for social activities; 33% of the centers reported parent involvement in raising funds for the center. At 41% of the centers, parents were not involved in any of these five ways. There were major differences between for-profit and nonprofit centers in the levels of parent participation, with higher percentages of nonprofit centers reporting parent participation in one or more of the modes studied. Among centers not receiving any government funds for any child, 67% of the profit centers indicated that parents were not involved in any of the five participation modes; this was the case at 36% of the nonprofit centers. Three percent of the profit and 22% of the nonprofit centers indicated that parents participated in staff selection. At 35% of the nonprofit centers but only 12% of the profit centers, parents reportedly were involved in reviewing budgets and programs. (See below for Powell [1978a] study of variations in parent-caregiver communication by proprietary status.)

If early childhood practitioners see their work as similar to the tasks of parenting, territoriality issues stemming from unclear role boundaries are likely to be a problem.

A limitation of the National Day Care Supply Study is that the above modes of participation were not examined in relation to opportunities for involvement. Presumably the centers included in the study represented modal versus model forms of child care, with a corresponding range of center policies and practices regarding parents. What type of participation exists when centers encourage or do not encourage parental presence at the center? A partial answer to this question comes from an observational study of parent participation in a laboratory child care center heavily committed to the principle of parent involvement. Zigler and Turner (1982) measured the absolute amount of time parents spent at a center that encouraged, but did not require, parent participation, visitation, and observation. Located at a Southwestern university, the center subscribed to an "open door" policy, offered monthly meetings on a variety of topics, and provided opportunities for conferences with teachers after hours. The investigators recorded the actual amount of time each parent of 50 target children was present at the center during a period of 70 consecutive days. Time recorded included the time parents spent dropping off or picking up their child, conferences with center staff, observation of children, and participation in group meetings.

Zigler and Turner found that parents spent an average of 7.4 minutes a day in the center, although there was considerable variation in the range of time spent at the center. For example, one mother (of a nursing infant) spent between 25 and 60 minutes at lunch time with her child on more than one-half of the 70 observation days. At the other extreme, 10% of the parents did not enter the center with their children in the morning, even though an unenforced policy called for parents to remain with their child during a health check. Another 10% of the children typically were brought to the center by someone other than a family member. During the 70-day observation period there were three parent conferences with teachers lasting no more than 10 minutes each. About one-half of the parents spent at least one hour on one or more occasions observing their child and his/her activities at the center. Forty percent of the parents of infants and toddlers dropped in during the day on one or more occasions to visit or play with their child; only 8% of parents of older children did so.

Head Start. As noted in Chapter 1, the Head Start performance standards mandate programs to provide opportunities for parent participation in decisions about program planning and operations; classrooms and other program activities as volunteers, observers, or paid employees; activities that parents themselves have helped to develop (e.g., parent education meeting); and working with their own children in cooperation with a program staff member.

To what degree do parents participate in Head Start programs? The Head Start Synthesis Project concluded that "sizable proportions" of parents participate in various paid and volunteer capacities. According to the report, the extent of involvement is uneven, with "a core of parents contributing a disproportionate share of time" (McKey et al., 1985, p. 17).

The National Head Start Parent Involvement study, which involved interviews with personnel from 30 randomly selected centers, found that a high percentage of Head Start programs provided parent involvement opportunities (Stubbs, 1980). Current and former Head Start parents comprised 89% of the centers' policymaking councils, for example, and 95% of the programs made budgetary provisions for parent-initiated activities. Seventy-seven percent of the programs used parent volunteers in the classrooms. A 1982–1983 annual survey of program operations indicated that 29% of the staff in all Head Start programs were parents of children in the program (Maxima Corporation, 1983).

The U.S. Comptroller General's 1975 report to Congress (cited in McKey et al., 1985) points to the uneven nature of program participation across Head Start parents. In the six programs studied, most parents had volunteered for at least a few hours each year. On the average, parents volunteered 32 hours a year, but 35% of the parents accounted for 71% of the total time volunteered. Four grantees kept records on parent attendance at center meetings. In two programs, 46% of the parents attended more than 50% of the meetings, while in the other two programs only 17% of the parents attended more than 50% of the meetings. There are indications a skewed distribution of program participation across parents persists today. The recent Commissioner's Task Force on Parent Involvement in Head Start recommended that Head Start develop a policy requiring parents to be involved in program operations a minimum number of hours a month.

Even though parents constitute a significant proportion of the local Head Start policy council, a historical assessment of Head Start policies and practices regarding parent involvement suggests that the political organizing role originally envisioned for Head Start parents has diminished, and an emphasis on parent education has come to dominate the Head Start parent involvement component (Valentine & Stark, 1979).

Mode, content, and frequency of communication

One of the first major studies of relations between parents and staff in early childhood programs was conducted by Powell (1977, 1978a, 1978b) in Detroit, Michigan. The sample was drawn from 12 full-day child care centers, yielding a total of 212 parents and 89 caregivers. Each of the

Even though parents constitute a significant portion of the local Head Start policy council, a historical assessment of Head Start policies and practices regarding parent involvement suggests that the political organizing role originally envisioned for Head Start parents has diminished, and an emphasis on parent education has come to dominate the Head Start parent involvement component.

Often the greatest parent/staff communication occurs when parents leave and retrieve their child at the center.

---

centers enrolled between 30 and 60 children from the ages of 2.5 to 5 years, and had been in operation for at least two years at the time of the study. Overall, the parent sample was 53% Afro-American and 45% Caucasian; 45% were working class, the remainder middle class, as determined by education and income level. Slightly more than one-half of the sample represented single-parent households, and a majority (69%) of all parents were using a child care center for the first time. The caregiver sample was 38% Afro-American and 58% Caucasian. Thirty-six percent had three to five years of formal experience in working with young children, and 60% had been employed at the center for two or more years at the time of the study. Data were collected with a structured interview conducted in person.

The highest frequency of communication between parents and caregivers occurred at the "transition point" when parents left and retrieved their child at the center. Some 66% of parents reported discussions with caregivers during this transition time on a weekly or more frequent basis. However, 30% of the parents reported that they typically did not enter the center premises when leaving their child for the day. Conferences between parents and staff were infrequent and never used by one-fourth of the parents. Formal visits to homes by center staff rarely occurred. For nearly one-third of the parents, communication with center staff was carried out with two or more caregivers. The remaining parents communicated consistently with a particular teacher (29%) or with the center director (32%). The child was the primary source of information about center activities for about 36% of the parents. Other primary information sources included teachers (16%), the center director (14%), and aides (13%).

Parents and caregivers reported discussing child-related topics considerably more frequently than parent/family-related topics. What the child's day was like at the center was the most frequently discussed topic. At the other extreme, parent's friends were almost never discussed. Child-peer relations and child-caregiver relations were among the most frequently discussed topics in the child domain. The parent's job or school was the most frequently discussed parent-related topic.

There was a strong correlation between communication frequency and diversity ($r = .92$ for parents; $r = .91$ for caregivers), suggesting that an increase in parent-caregiver interaction corresponded to an increase in the diversity or range of discussion topics. To examine this relationship in more detail, three subgroups in each of the parent and caregiver samples were created on the basis of communication frequency (low, medium, high). Examination of differences between these subgroups indicated that each of the subgroups discussed child-related topics most frequently. As communication frequency increased, the number of family-related topics

It appears that a great many parents, probably about one-third, typically do not enter the center when leaving their child.

increased. Also, the number of statistically significant relationships among topics within the two topic domains (child, parent/family) increased with communication frequency. As frequency of communication increased, parent contact with the child care staff became increasingly focused on one particular caregiver; it was among parents with lower frequencies of communication with center staff that contact was spread among two or more caregivers. As communication frequency increased, then, so did the probability of a parent and caregiver forming and sustaining a consistent, stable relationship with one another.

Thus, it appeared that the core content of communication, clearly child-related, remained the same despite increases in communication frequency. However, as frequency increased, the content boundaries broadened to encompass family-related information. Further, as communication increased, topics related to children and those relating to parents and family became increasingly interrelated.

The Powell study also examined attitudes toward the content boundaries and levels of parent-caregiver communication. A majority of both parents (85%) and caregivers (92%) indicated that parents and caregivers should discuss the center's goals and general expectations, but considerably fewer parents (51%) and caregivers (64%) believed there should be discussion of parental suggestions for specific caregiver practices. A majority of parents (61%) and caregivers (53%) indicated the center should *not* be kept informed of family activities on a constant basis. About one-half of the parent sample but only 33% of the caregivers did not believe family problems should be discussed with center staff as a general principle. With regard to satisfaction, significantly more caregivers (72%) than parents (50%) were dissatisfied with the overall level of parent-caregiver communication as it existed at the time of the study. When asked about specific topics, however, most parents (77%) and caregivers (70%) were not satisfied with the existing level of discussion about the children's activities at the center. Interestingly, more than half (56%) of the parents but only one-quarter (26%) of the caregivers were satisfied with parent-staff communication regarding the child's home life. Also, more parents (58%) than caregivers (25%) were pleased with the level of discussion surrounding parental expectations of the center.

In a study of informal parent-staff communication in centers when parents picked up their children in the afternon, Winkelstein (1981) found that social communication (verbal greetings) occurred with greater frequency than informational communication (factual statements, e.g., "We are going on a field trip tomorrow") or decision-making communication (e.g., "I'd like to have the center try more fruit at snack time").

The most common responses to parent concerns by both center and home providers included: asking questions, offering sympathy, presenting alternatives, and just listening.

The data were collected through observations on two afternoons at four centers.

Data from parents indicate that interpersonal ties between parents and caregivers may be stronger in family day care than in center-based arrangements. A study of 126 parents in Victoria, British Columbia found that parents using family day care reported closer personal relationships with caregivers than parents using child care centers. Compared to users of center care, parents using family day care reported speaking with caregivers more often and were more likely to anticipate they would "keep in touch" with their child's caregiver after the child left the family day care home (Pence & Goelman, 1987).

Data from providers also point to differences between family day care and center providers in the frequency and duration of parent-provider discussions. In interviews with 73 providers representing 35 homes and 38 centers in a Midwestern community, Hughes (1985) found that center providers spent an average of 13.7 minutes per week while home providers spent 54.7 minutes per week with each parent. There were no differences between center and home providers in the types of concerns discussed with parents. These ranged from discussions of information and insight to major problems affecting physical or psychological health. The frequency with which some of these topics were discussed with parents differed, however. Center providers reported more frequent discussions than home providers about child-related topics of learning, social development, behavior problems, peer relationships, and policies. Home providers discussed relationships with relatives more frequently than center providers. For both provider groups, the parent's job was the most frequently mentioned topic of discussion, and problems with spouse were the least likely topic.

Hughes asked providers to describe the typical ways in which they responded to the concerns of parents (e.g., try to change the topic, give advice). Home providers were more likely than center providers to tell parents to count their blessings, while center providers were more likely to suggest that parents talk to someone else. The most common responses of both center and home providers included: asking questions, offering sympathy, presenting alternatives, and just listening.

Hughes suggests that differences between home and center providers in the frequency and content of discussions with parents may be a function of the setting. In comparison to family day care homes, the higher ratio of providers to children in centers translates into less available time for interaction with parents. Also, Hughes suggests it is not surprising that center providers discussed learning or educational progress with parents to a greater extent than home providers since most centers are likely to have a formal educational component in their program. Further, the greatest number of children in centers compared to homes may account for the more frequent discussions of behavior problems, social development, and peer relations with center parents.

The child's age also might account for some of the differences between center and home regarding frequency of parent-provider contact. Children in family day care homes typically are younger than the children enrolled in centers. As noted earlier in this section, Zigler and Turner (1982) found that parents of infants and toddlers were present at the center more frequently than parents of older children. However, in the previously mentioned Pence and Goelman (1987) study, which found stronger parent-provider ties in family day care than in center care, children were between the ages of 2½ and 5 years in both types of care.

The findings from the Hughes (1985) study and other investigations provide evidence of supportive relationships involving active helping behaviors in child care settings. In a study of Berkeley, California, preschool programs, Joffe (1977) discovered a viable program "underlife" where staff provided a range of informal services negotiated privately between parents and staff members. The activities included after-school chauffeuring, legal and medical advice, and career counseling. Hughes (1985) notes that the helping responses the child care providers in his study reported were more active than the strategies of informal helpers examined in other investigations. For example, as informal helpers, hairdressers and bartenders have been found to be sympathetic, lighthearted, and willing to listen to the concerns of their clients (Cowen et al., 1979). The Hughes data on informal helping relationships are from the perspective of providers, leaving unanswered the question of how parents react to the help offered by their child's caregiver. Whether these helping exchanges involve a minority or majority of parents also is unclear. In the Powell study, about one-fourth of the caregivers reported that they considered some of their parents to be friends. Caregiver interaction with these parent-friends occurred on a weekly or more frequent basis in settings other than the child care center (e.g., church). Topics discussed included job/school, childrearing issues, family activities and problems, and the child care center.

Uses and potential misuses of information

What are the anticipated uses of information exchanged between parents and teachers? For instance, toward what end does a teacher tell a parent about a child's day at the center? A small-scale, exploratory study involving in-depth interviews with early childhood teachers in half-day nursery schools, full-day child care centers, and Head Start programs uncovered three distinct teacher expectations for the ways parents use information provided by teachers (Powell & Stremmel, 1987).

One hope of teachers in this study was that parents would develop positive feelings about the center and the child's classroom experiences. Teachers wanted parents to trust them and to view the center as a stimulating setting for their child. A second expectation was that parents would use teacher-provided information to reinforce the child's classroom learnings. For example, when a teacher posted a report of the week's curriculum activities on the bulletin board or told a parent, "Today we focused on *G* words," often it was with the expectation that the parent would continue the lesson or topic at home. Third, teachers expected that parents might alter or refine their perceptions of and/or interactions with the child. Some of the teachers in this study believed that parents hold inappropriate expectations regarding their child's development, and hence the teachers reportedly sought to change parental cognitions or behaviors where deemed inappropriate. Consider the following practice described by a teacher interviewed in the study:

> If a child puts on her coat for me at recess but demands that her parent put it on when it's time to go home, I casually tell the parent about the child's accomplishments with the coat while at school. I don't say anything about the parent putting on the coat. I simply offer information about the child's capabilities. (Powell & Stremmel, 1987, p. 118)

Equally illustrative here is the response of a teacher to a parent who reportedly commented to the teacher, "Every time I pick up Eric he's playing by himself. I wish he'd play more with others" (Powell & Stremmel, 1987, p. 122). The teacher's six-word response — "That's just the way Eric is" — communicated the teacher's acceptance of the child's behaviors and indirectly questioned the parent's desire for the child to have more peer involvement. In this instance, the intent of the teacher was to help broaden the parent's understanding of "normal" child behavior and development.

What uses do teachers make of information provided by parents? Overwhelmingly, teachers interviewed in the Powell and Stremmel study indicated that they might use parent-provided information about the child to enhance interactions with the child. If an out-of-town relative is visiting and a child seems particularly excited, for example, a teacher would talk with the child about the relative's visit. Teachers also reported using parent-provided information to generate inferences about the causes of child behavior. In some instances it appeared this was a defensive posture on the part of teachers. Noted one teacher in the study: "Any negative behavior from the child is usually blamed on the day care by many parents. Knowing what's going on at home usually helps me realize it's not the day care's fault." A third use was to monitor parents' perceptions of the child

In communicating with parents, teachers expect the information they provide (1) to get parents to trust them and to view the center as a stimulating setting for their child, (2) to help parents reinforce the child's classroom learnings at home, and (3) to alter or refine parents' perceptions and/or interactions with the child.

A critical question is whether parents hear seemingly covert
messages in the way they are intended.

care program, including judgments of the staff. Teachers were troubled by
the absence of information from parents. It was difficult for staff to
determine whether parental silence reflected a lack of interest in the
program and/or the child, or a lack of trust in the center staff.

A critical question is whether parents hear seemingly covert messages in
the way they are intended:

> A teacher who makes the observation, "Your child put on her coat by herself
> today so well," intends to inform or remind the parent of child skills the
> parent is not encouraging, at least during parent-child interactions at the
> early childhood program. However, there are several other logical interpreta-
> tions a parent might apply to the teacher's comment: "The teacher can get
> my child to do things I can't. The teacher's better than I am. The teacher
> must think I'm a bad mother." Or, "Why does my child do things for the
> teacher that she doesn't do for me? There must be something wrong with my
> relationship with my child." Presumably these are not interpretations a
> teacher would want a parent to apply to the comment. Yet the covert intent
> of the statement provides considerable latitude of the parent in determining
> the teacher's intent. (Powell & Stremmel, 1987, p. 125)

This study's exploration of teacher's intentions for parental use of
teacher-provided information points to the potentially important role of
informal parent education within early childhood programs. In addition to
the casual and more formal staff comments to parents, there is a rich
opportunity to observe a range of child behaviors and styles of adult-child
interaction at drop-off and pickup times. Whether parents perceive the
setting to be an information resource seems variable, however. In the
Detroit study of parent-caregiver communication (Powell, 1978b), about
60% of the parents perceived the child care center as a source of information about childrearing. More research is needed on the process and effects
of the informal parent education function of early childhood centers.

Perceptions of parenting abilities

Parent and caregiver perceptions of their own and each other's childrearing competence represent a component of relations between parents and
early childhood staff. This section describes what is known about attitudes
toward parents' parenting abilities.

Susan Kontos and her colleagues have conducted a series of investigations on the attitudes of caregivers and parents toward parent childrearing competence. The attitudinal measure involves asking respondents to
rate each of 30 items in relation to (1) their own standards of good parenting practices, (2) how typical the item is of parents using the center
(or of parents themselves), and (3) how typical the item is of most
American parents.

Staff attitudes toward center parents may be part of a general negative outlook toward parents, which is improved slightly in the context of the center relationship.

In a questionnaire study of 236 early childhood staff representing full-day child care, Head Start, and preschool programs in two Midwestern states, center staff rated the childrearing practices of their center parents lower than their own (staff) standards of good parenting but higher than most parents today (Kontos, Raikes, & Woods, 1983). The finding suggests that staff attitudes toward center parents may be part of a general negative outlook toward parents, which is improved slightly in the context of the center relationship. In a subsequent study involving 47 caregivers and 110 parents, Kontos (1984) found that parents rated their own behavior as similar to their standards of good parenting. Consistent with the findings of the earlier Kontos et al. (1983) investigation, child care staff in the latter study indicated negative attitudes toward both parents using the caregiver's services and most parents today. Parents also expressed negative attitudes toward the childrearing practices of most parents today. The overall picture, then, is one in which parents and staff seem to share similar ideals for good parenting as well as negative judgments regarding the practices of most American parents today, but differ significantly in how close they perceive center parents approach ideal parenting practices.

These data raise questions about the accuracy and source of caregiver judgments regarding the childrearing abilities of their parent clientele. The accuracy question stems from the finding that caregivers perceive much larger discrepancies between ideal and actual parenting among center parents than the parents themselves perceive. Also, knowing the source of information caregivers use to form opinions of parents may prove helpful in the design of efforts to enhance staff relations with parents.

Research conducted by Kontos and Dunn (in press) provides some answers to these questions. The study investigated differences in mothers whose childrearing abilities were held in high versus low esteem by caregivers. The sample included 100 3- to 5-year-old children from 10 child care centers in northeastern Pennsylvania. The findings suggest that caregiver perceptions of parents' childrearing ability are related to children's developmental outcomes, mothers' experiences with child care, childrearing values, and demographic characteristics. Specifically, children of mothers whose parenting practices caregivers held in low esteem were lower in cognitive, language, and social development than children of mothers held in high esteem. Low-group mothers reported fewer communications with child care staff: for example, 50% of high-group mothers compared to 17% of low-group mothers reported daily communication with center staff. Low-group mothers were less likely to think that someone from their center was familiar with the entire family's activities. Although the entire sample was generally satisfied with the center and reported few

*There are suggestions in the literature that teachers'
stereotypes of socioeconomic and racial subgroups influence
staff perceptions of parenting competence.*

problems with center staff, the low-group mothers were less satisfied with their center than high-group mothers, and if problems arose, they were primarily over center rules and regulations. Further, low-group mothers more highly valued conformity in their children and were more likely to be divorced than high-group mothers. An earlier, smaller study by Kontos and Wells (1986) discovered similar differences between low- and high-group mothers regarding single parent status, limited communication with caregivers, restrictive childrearing values, and conflicts with center staff over center rules and regulations.

These findings add credence to the notion that caregiver judgments regarding parenting competence are related to reliable differences in parental behaviors and attitudes. The data also lend themselves to speculations as to what information sources caregivers use to form their opinions. Child behaviors could be a primary source of influence on caregiver judgments. Caregivers may be observing developmental lags in the children of low-group mothers and inferring poorer childrearing abilities on the part of their mothers. In this scenario, caregivers may use child behavior at the center to assess the nature of home life. Direct observation of parental behavior also could contribute to caregiver judgments. Kontos and Dunn (in press) speculate that caregivers may observe less than optimal childrearing on the part of the mothers held in low esteem. These mothers may exhibit parenting behaviors that reflect their value of conformity in children, as well as stress or role overload due to their combined status as a single and working parent.

The nature of parent-caregiver communication also warrants consideration as a determinant of caregiver judgments. Overall, low-group mothers had significantly less contact with center staff on a daily basis and hence may have been perceived as less interested in their child and/or the center. Recall this chapter's earlier discussion of teachers' struggles in interpreting parental silence (Powell & Stremmel, 1987). Caregivers may feel more warmly toward those with whom they have frequent contact and discuss shared concerns or topics. It appears from the Kontos and Dunn study that parental conflicts with center staff may not be a major source of caregiver judgments since relatively few parents reported instances of conflict or disagreement.

There are suggestions in the literature that teachers' stereotypes of socioeconomic and racial subgroups influence staff perceptions of parenting competence. Lightfoot's (1978) case study of a first-grade teacher revealed stereotypic images of low-income, working-class, and professional occupation groups that guided the teacher's interactions with parents, for instance. The Kontos and Dunn data indirectly question the influence

There are strong beliefs in this country that families and young children suffer when mothers of young children work out of the home.

---

of socioeconomic group stereotypes on caregiver judgments. There were no differences between low and high groups in education, occupation, income, or Hollingshead Index of socioeconomic status. Whether caregivers' subjective impressions of parents' social status coincide with objective measures of socioeconomic status cannot be determined from this study.

The generally positive views of parents toward the center might suggest that parents held in low esteem by caregivers were unaware of the negative staff attitudes. Perhaps staff interacted with parents with a professional demeanor that failed to reveal their true feelings. Also, because low-group mothers communicated less frequently with staff, there were few opportunities for staff to reveal their judgmentalness (Kontos, 1987). For a definitive understanding of links between staff attitudes and behaviors regarding parents, we need research on parent-staff interactions and on parents' understandings of how staff view them. In Epstein's (1984a, 1985) large study of parent involvement at the elementary school level, teachers who did not emphasize parent involvement made more demands on single parents for helping their child at home and rated single parents as less helpful and responsible on activities at home than married parents. Parents with less education also reported significantly more frequent requests from teachers for helping at home than did parents with average or advanced levels of education. In contrast, teachers who emphasized parent involvement made equal demands on all parents, regardless of marital or education status, to help their children at home. They also rated single and married parents as equally helpful and responsible.

Parents' views of early childhood staff's competence have not been examined with the detail pursued in the Kontos investigations of staff judgments of parents. Elementary school teachers have been found to rate their own competence significantly higher than do mothers and fathers, for instance (Power, 1985). In early childhood programs, empirical data on parental views of staff competence might enhance our current asymmetrical understanding of how parent and staff perceptions of each other's competence contribute to relations between families and programs.

Separation and attachment feelings

Maternal separation from the child and caregiver attachment to the child are important elements of shared childrearing experiences. There are indications in the literature that these adult feelings may contribute to the quality of the parent-caregiver relationship.

Several studies have given attention to the psychological dimensions of parents' experiences surrounding a child's transition from home to school

At the same time, a contemporary cultural sentiment is that women who remain at home to care for children are weak intellectually ("just a mother").

or nonfamilial care setting. An early study on this topic found that, upon entrance into kindergarten, mothers experienced a sense of displacement, including anxiety and tension regarding the child's relationship with the teacher (Klein & Ross, 1958). Currently, "the other woman" (Lightfoot, 1978) enters the lives of many children much earlier than kindergarten. Anecdotal information indicates that parents report a range of strong emotions on their child's first day in a child care setting: nervous, anxious, sad, worried, apprehensive, tense, strange, lost (Balaban, 1985).

A mother's apprehensions about leaving her child with a nonfamilial caregiver can lead to an unpleasant emotional state that Ellen Hock has labeled *maternal separation anxiety* (Hock, 1984; Hock, DeMeis, & McBride, 1988; Hock, McBride, & Gnezda, in press). Expressions of this anxiety include feelings of sadness, worry, or uneasiness about being away from the child. Hock and her colleagues have examined this psychological variable in relation to infant adjustment to child care (Hock, 1984) and employment preferences and choices about nonfamilial child care (Hock et al., 1988).

Hock et al. (1988) found that employed mothers who experienced anxiety in terms of their perception of separation effects on the child were less likely to enroll their child in a child care center. For these mothers, the typical child care arrangement was a sitter in parent's home or a family day care setting. For nonemployed mothers, higher scores on the scale measuring maternal perceptions of separation effects on the child were associated with a pattern of decreased use of preschool; that is, nonemployed mothers with greater concern about the effects of separation on the child had their child enrolled in fewer days of preschool per week than nonemployed mothers with less concern about separation effects. The power of this psychological variable is suggested in the Hock et al. longitudinal finding that mothers who, in the maternity ward, expressed higher levels of concern about leaving a baby to return to work were less likely to enroll their 3-year-olds in preschool. This is surprising in view of the many demographic and life circumstance factors that strongly influence preschool attendance.

It has been argued that current societal norms about motherhood intensify the level of emotional stress mothers experience when they leave their young child in the care of another (Gerson, Alpert, & Richardson, 1984; McCartney & Phillips, 1988; Hock et al., 1988). There are strong beliefs in this country that families and young children suffer when mothers of young children work out of the home. At the same time, a contemporary cultural sentiment is that women who remain at home to care for children are weak intellectually ("just a mother").

Guilt is one manifestation of this conflicting set of messages about the ideal motherhood role in America today. In case study interviews with six women of various occupations and childrearing arrangements, McCartney and Phillips (1988, pp. 173–175) identified three beliefs associated with the guilt theme. One belief is that working outside the home will disrupt the mother's role as primary caregiver (". . . you need to commit time for a child's growth, especially from 2 to 5. . . . One day I hope I won't feel regret for having worked this time"). Another is that it will prevent observation of the child's important developmental accomplishments ("I realized how much I was going to miss—her first step, her first tooth"). A third belief is that it will adversely affect others' attitudes about a woman's mothering abilities ("People let you know in subtle and not so subtle ways that you will never be mother of the year").

It is not clear how maternal feelings of guilt or separation anxiety are connected to the relationship between mothers and early childhood staff. Perhaps mothers who feel possessive of their unique relationship with the child come to resent or feel envious of the time the child spends with a caregiver. Hock's data would suggest that if maternal separation anxiety is a factor in the parent-caregiver relationship, it is likely to be more pronounced among parents using family day care and providers in the parent's home than among parents using a center.

Perceptions of staff competence also may be involved. Informal interviews with parents suggest that parental trust of the early childhood staff reduces anxious feelings about separating from the child (e.g., "I felt that he was in good hands," Balaban, 1985, p. 10). In a study of employed mothers of infants and toddlers in child care centers, Mann and Thornburg (1987) found that mothers who reported more satisfaction with child care also reported feeling less guilt about leaving their child in out-of-home care. Interestingly, mothers who reported more satisfaction with home-school communication reported feeling more guilt. Perhaps there was an increased level of information about the child's daily activities that prompted mothers to feel they were missing key developmental changes in their child's life.

Early childhood teachers' experiences with attachment to and separation from children placed in their care apparently have not commanded the interest of researchers. There are anecdotal reports of child care staff making negative comments about parents after six weeks of working with a child ("That mother is feeding her child junk food," Galinsky, 1988, p. 9). Galinsky has interpreted these complaints as positive signs of teachers becoming attached to the children, but also as an indication that help may be needed to prevent staff complaints from turning into rivalries for the child's affection.

Mothers who report more satisfaction with child care also report feeling less guilt about leaving their child in out-of-home care.

Parents want praise *for their childrearing practices. They look to other adults with whom the child has contact for affirmation of their parenting competence.*

In view of current cultural norms about motherhood, it seems plausible that for early childhood staff a source of tension in the parent-staff relationship may be the perception that mothers who work outside of the home indirectly defy the caregiver's chosen role of working with young children (see Galinsky, 1988). Caregivers may believe that a parent who leaves a young child in the care of other adults in order to pursue work is suggesting that the caregiver's job of being with young children is not very important. This factor has not been examined systematically but warrants research attention in the context of existing societal norms.

Relationship preferences

Parents and early childhood teachers seem to enter the staff-parent relationship with needs or preferences for how the relationship should work. Carole Joffe (1977) gave particular attention to this aspect of the program-family intersection in her ethnographic study of publicly funded nursery schools in Berkeley, California.

Parents want *praise* for their childrearing practices. They look to other adults with whom the child has contact for affirmation of their parenting competence. When children participate in public settings such as child care centers, parents "go public" with their childrearing skills. The arena enables caregivers and other parents to view the quality of parent-child interaction and, perhaps inappropriately, to use informal observations of child behavior to make inferences about the home environment. In Joffe's study, some parents experienced fear that perceived child misbehavior at the center would constitute public exposure as an incompetent parent. Galinsky (1981) also encountered the parental need for feedback on childrearing skills in her interview study of parenthood stages. A mother of a 3-year-old told Galinsky of her need to receive "an A plus in parenthood" from her child's teacher. She wanted "to be told in no uncertain terms that I had a fabulous child who had been raised to be a delight in school" (p. 158).

Parents also want staff to *implement their images of appropriate program experiences for young children.* Joffe discovered important differences between Afro-American and Caucasian parents in expectations of early childhood programs. Afro-American parents preferred a more formal school atmosphere with respect to discipline, structuring of activity, and academic curriculum, whereas Caucasian parents desired a program emphasizing social, emotional, and intellectual qualities of children. The Caucasian parents' interest in the program activities pertaining to intellectual stimulation was ambiguous; the preference seemed to be for the program to meet the child's intellectual needs but not through a traditional academic

What do staff want from parents? Existing studies point to autonomy and support. *Occupational groups that wish to improve or maintain their professional status generally seek detachment from the lay public.*

program. Joffe observed that the conflict in these differing parental expectations appeared to be resolved through a "symbolic trade-off" whereby Afro-American parents were successful in securing an educational curriculum, but Caucasian preferences dominated the "tone" or interpersonal style of the program (e.g., no corporal punishment and daily scheduling of activities in spontaneous and informal ways).

Some parents in Joffe's study desired opportunities for parents to pursue *personal and professional development interests.* Nearly all parents indicated they had gained new friendships through the early childhood program. Formal and informal discussions at an early childhood program enable parents to form meaningful ties with peers experiencing a common life circumstance. Some parents also pursued the chance to develop or refine career-related skills. One parent, for instance, photographed young children at the center and eventually opened her own studio; another parent published a cookbook for children.

What do staff want from parents? Existing studies point to *autonomy and support.* Occupational groups that wish to improve or maintain their professional status generally seek detachment from the lay public; it is the professional, not the client, who defines the presenting problem and prescribes a remedy (see Joffe, 1977; Powell, 1982). It is of little surprise, then, to find that teachers define "good parents" as those who abide by the teacher's rules and avoid interference in the classroom (Lortie, 1975). Joffe uncovered instances of early childhood teachers' efforts to create and sustain professional distance from parents. In a meeting about whether to continue in-service work on developmental theories, for example, one teacher indicated that she wanted to study Erikson and other theorists not because the information helped her in teaching but because the knowledge made her feel "authoritative" in dealing with parents: "When they challenge me on something, I'll just throw Erikson at them" (Joffe, 1977, p. 49). In a similar vein, a teacher interviewed in the Powell and Stremmel (1987) study indicated that "if the Board of Directors told me parents would be writing the curriculum, I would find that a hard pill to swallow" (p. 120).

While the autonomy theme is strong in the literature, it is counterbalanced by staff desire for parental support. At least four types of support can be discerned. As noted earlier, teachers want parents to be responsive to staff suggestions and advice regarding parental interactions and activities with the child. This reflects a larger staff expectation or hope for family activities that support and extend center philosophy and practices. Teachers also desire information from parents that helps staff understand a child's background and current home life situation. Third, some teachers seek an appropriate level of involvement in center activities from parents. In the Powell and Stremmel study, "appropriate" participation meant parents sharing talents or skills in the classroom but generally toward curriculum goals and activities established by teachers. Joffe describes several incidents in which strong parental interest in a matter related to the early childhood center (e.g., natural foods, sexism, center beautification) led to what some staff considered to be overinvolvement, with attendant annoyance to staff and other parents. Lastly, early childhood staff want support from parents in the form of program advocacy. Speaking at public hearings, writing letters to elected officials regarding early childhood issues, and securing funds for program operations were important activities parents collaboratively pursued with staff at the centers Joffe studied.

Some early childhood workers may take steps to establish staff authority and parental support at the time parents inquire about the program. Some teachers in the Powell and Stremmel exploratory study told of efforts to communicate center goals clearly to parents prior to the enrollment of the child, and strongly encouraged parents to visit classrooms and talk with teachers about their practices. The teachers seemed to desire a self-selection process here by implicitly stating, "What we do with children may not be what you want. Find out before you make a commitment." Powell and Stremmel interpreted this up-front communication strategy as serving to (a) establish the teacher's authority regarding curriculum matters; (b) generate a parent clientele that would be supportive of program philosophy and practice; and thereby (c) minimize potential parent criticism of the program or requests for different approaches.

Variations in staff-parent relations

What factors are predictive of differences in relations between parents and early childhood staff? Several investigators have attempted to answer this question by examining personal and organizational characteristics.

Demographic and attitudinal variables have been found to be associated with the nature of ties between parents and child care workers. With regard to communication, the Detroit study (Powell, 1977) found four variables to be predictive of the frequency of parent communication with center staff: the attitude that parents and caregivers should discuss family information; active participation in an informal social network of parents using the same center; use of the center for six months or less; and membership in a two-parent family. These variables accounted for about 24% of the variance in frequency of parent communication with center staff. In the Zigler and Turner (1982) study, however, marital status and length of child care use were not predictive of the amount of time parents were present at the child care center. Zigler and Turner found increases in the amount of time spent at the center to be associated with smaller families (i.e., number of children), younger children, and lower income. Together these variables accounted for 16% of the variance in parental time spent at the center.

The Powell study found the following variables to be predictive of the frequency of caregiver communication: center role function (i.e., directors talked with parents more than teachers did); recent completion of formal education; little formal experience in working with young children; a child-centered role concept; and the attitude that childrearing values should be discussed with parents. These variables accounted for about 48% of the variance in caregiver communication frequency. In Hughes's (1985) study, the provider's age was positively correlated with discussion of parent issues (parent's job, marital problems, feelings of depression), suggesting that perhaps parents felt more comfortable talking about themselves with older individuals. Older providers used less active helping responses (e.g., just listening, telling parents to count their blessings). More highly educated providers reported a higher frequency of discussing social development and child learning topics with parents than providers with less formal education, whereas providers with more years of experience reported a higher frequency of discussing child discipline and physical growth with parents.

One of the first quantitative studies of family day care arrangements found that satisfaction and stress varied in relation to whether the provider was a friend or a stranger to the parent at the outset of the family day care arrangement (Emlen, Donoghue, & LaForge, 1971). In arrangements between women who had known each other before the arrangement began, the friendship was the bond that held the arrangement together. Strains in the day care arrangements between friends seemed to involve problems of status, dominance, definition of expectations, and renegotiation of interpersonal relationships. Emlen et al. suggest that the use of a friend or prior acquaintance as a regular caregiver may introduce status discrepancies that are incompatible with the equality characteristic of friendships. When friendships were strong, parent and caregiver satisfactions with the arrangement were high. However, when there was prior acquaintance without a high degree of friendship, negotiation of the boundaries and expectations for the relationship and the arrangement became sources of tension.

The Powell study was designed to examine the relation of center sponsorship (proprietary, nonproprietary) to communication frequency. Analyses yielded no differences in parent or caregiver communicative behavior and attitudes in relation to the for-profit or nonprofit status of centers.

Summary

Sociological treatments of home-school relations have emphasized the unique characteristics of families and secondary socialization agencies, including the distinctive roles of parents and teachers, and pointed to the inevitability of parent-teacher conflict. Theorists have called for optimal social distance between families and secondary childrearing institutions, arguing that collaboration is necessary but a lack of boundary maintenance would jeopardize each setting's special roles and characteristics. An analysis of this theoretical approach points to limited applicability to early childhood settings because of the wide scope of functions generally found in most child care settings due to the young age of the child. Hence, the work of early childhood practitioners is likely to be viewed as similar to the tasks of parenting, resulting in unclear role boundaries that may fuel territoriality issues.

Few studies offer a profile of the patterns of parental participation in early childhood programs. A massive 1976–1977 survey of a national probability sample of full-day child care centers in the United States found that a majority offered parents counseling on child development, but only one-third also offered a range of other family support services. At a majority of centers, parents were not involved in reviewing budgets and programs, staff selection, volunteer capacities, social activities, or fund raising. A study of parental presence at a university-based child care center committed to parent involvement found that parents spent an average of 7.4 minutes a day at the center. With regard to Head Start, studies indicate that sizable proportions of parents participate in various paid and volunteer activities, but a core of parents is involved a disproportionate share of the time.

Studies of child care centers reveal that the highest frequency of parent-staff communication occurred when parents leave and retrieve their child at the center. Parent-teacher conferences and staff visits to the child's home were infrequent or nonexistent. Child-related topics were discussed with greater frequency than parent- or family-related topics, and increases in parent-staff interaction were related to increases in the diversity or range of topics discussed. Even though the child's day at the center was the most frequently discussed topic, a vast majority of both parents and caregivers were dissatisfied with the level of parent-caregiver discussion regarding activities at the center. Parents and caregivers were in disagreement about the appropriateness of parents discussing family problems with center staff, and more caregivers than parents were dissatisfied with the existing level of parent-staff communication.

Findings of several studies suggest that interpersonal ties between parents and caregivers may be stronger in family day care arrangements than in center-based settings. Family day care providers spend more time talking with parents than center providers do. There are indications that both center and family child care providers offer active helping responses to parental concerns and problems.

Exploratory research on teachers' intentions in communications with parents suggests that staff want parents to develop positive, trusting feelings about the center; reinforce program philosophy and curriculum at home; and refine or expand their understanding of child development and perceptions of their child in particular. Parent education may occur informally in early childhood settings through daily exchanges between parents and staff. Exploratory data suggest that many staff messages to parents may be covert or subtle, raising questions as to whether parents hear staff comments in the manner in which they are intended.

Center staff have been found to rate the childrearing practices of their center parents lower than their own (staff) standards of good parenting but higher than the practices of most American parents today. Parents rated their own behavior as similar to their own standards of good parenting and, like caregivers, expressed negative attitudes toward most American parents today. Caregiver judgments regarding parenting competence appear to be related to reliable differences in parental behaviors and attitudes. Mothers whose parenting skills were held in low esteem by caregivers had children with lower cognitive, language, and social development than that of children of mothers held in high esteem. Also, low-group mothers reported fewer communications with child care staff and were generally less satisfied with the center than high-group mothers. Mothers held in low esteem by caregivers were more likely to be single parents and to value conformity in their children than high-esteem mothers. The sources of information that influence caregiver judgments about parents are not clear, but possibilities include inferences based on work with the child, the infrequent nature of parent-caregiver communication, and observations of parental behavior with the child.

There is little research information about maternal separation anxiety and caregiver attachment to the child as possible influences on the parent-staff relationship. Studies have found employed mothers who experienced anxiety regarding separation effects on the child were less likely to enroll their child in a child care center, and nonemployed mothers with greater concern about separation effects on the child enrolled their child in fewer days of preschool per week. Anecdotal reports suggest that parental perceptions of staff competence may reduce anxious feelings about separation from the child.

Ethnographic data suggest that parents want the following from early childhood settings: praise for their childrearing practices; an implementation of their images of appropriate program experiences for young children; and (among some parents) opportunities to pursue personal and professional development interests. It appears that early childhood staff want autonomy from parental control of classroom activities, but also support from parents in the form of responsiveness to staff suggestions, information about the child's background and home life, an appropriate level of involvement in center activities, and program advocacy.

Effects of parent participation in early childhood programs

The foregoing description of adult experiences in early childhood programs leads to the obvious question of whether the program-parent relationship affects the growth and development of the adult participants, the programs through which they are connected, or the institutions of the community in which parents also might be involved. Chapter 1 delineated these anticipated outcomes of program-parent interaction in the following manner: parent's self-development; responsiveness of community-based human service institutions; and program resources. (Effects on children were described in Chapter 2.)

There is limited research information on the extent to which these anticipated outcomes have been realized. The outcomes have been examined in relation to parent participation in program operations, and not in connection with the frequency of parent-staff communication or other relationship dimensions independent of a particular mode of program involvement. The bulk of the studies has focused on the effects of parents' program decision-making and classroom volunteer roles. Further, most of the studies have been conducted with low-income or working-class populations in community-based early childhood programs such as Head Start.

Parent's self-development

Self-development is a general label subsuming a variety of behaviors and attitudes that proponents of family-program collaboration have argued are results of parent participation. It includes such attributes as education levels, attitudes toward education, feelings of competence and self-worth, and financial independence. These outcomes pertain to the parent as person, and not to the parent as childrearer.

There is some evidence that low-income parents involved for a number of years in high-quality child care or Head Start programs feel less powerless in their children's lives.

A 10-year follow-up study of the effects of an intensive early intervention program for impoverished mothers and their children found positive program effects on mothers' financial self-sufficiency and education levels (Seitz, Rosenbaum, & Apfel, 1985). The program involved a high-quality child care center plus medical and social services provided to mothers in an individualized manner. Ten years after program completion, almost all of the program participants but only half of the mothers in the control group were self-supporting, and program participants had completed significantly more years of post-secondary education than control group mothers. Program participants had markedly fewer children than the control group mothers did.

Positive program effects on parents were found in a study of a high-quality child care program for children of low-income parents (Ramey, Dorval, & Baker-Ward, 1983). After approximately five years of child care involvement, mothers of children in care, when compared to control mothers, were less likely to say they were powerless to influence the schools and that teacher is not the parent's job (Schaefer, cited in Ramey et al., 1983). Whether interactions with the child care program or some other variable (for example, participation in the work force) contributed to these differences is not clear.

At least one study of Head Start program effects discovered increased levels of education among program participants (Adams, 1976). However, the literature reviewed for the Head Start Synthesis Project indicated that Head Start has little effect on changing parents' attitudes toward the value of education. Most studies could find no attitudinal difference between Head Start and non-Head Start parents (McKey et al., 1985).

There is some indication in the Head Start evaluation literature that the program affects parent's attitudes toward their own lives, but there are insufficient data to ascertain whether the program is the causal element. For example, a pretest/posttest study of the relation of psychological well-being to participation in Head Start found a positive relationship: Mothers who participated more often reported fewer psychological symptoms, greater feelings of mastery, and greater current life satisfaction at the end of the program (Parker, Piotrkowski, & Peay, 1987). The Head Start Synthesis Project offered the following summary of findings of studies on this topic:

> Several studies suggest that mothers who actively participate in Head Start are happier and show increased trust in other people, improved psychological well-being, and less anxiety, depression and somatic complaints than mothers who participate less. There is not enough information, however, to be sure that Head Start experience is the cause of those positive outcomes. (McKey et al., 1985, p. 18)

Among the anecdotal reports in the literature are numerous illustrations of Head Start parents having direct impact on medical services and public school systems.

Human service institutions

Do relations between parents and staff in early childhood programs help parents develop skills in dealing with human service institutions that enable parents to make institutions in their community more responsive to their needs? This is a methodologically difficult question to examine, but there is some evidence to suggest that early childhood programs can function as a training ground for parents to learn how to participate in other institutional settings. Whether this knowledge in turn contributes to changes in other community institutions cannot be determined from the existing data.

One indication that early childhood programs may provide parents with competencies in dealing with other institutions comes from the previously discussed Seitz et al. (1985) 10-year follow-up of early intervention program effects. The study found that program mothers were more likely to assume an active stance in dealing with their child's school than mothers in the control group. Ten years after program termination, program mothers were more likely to have initiated contact with their child's teacher in the previous year, whereas control group mothers had a pattern of relating to the school in response to a teacher's request for contact. Seitz et al. have hypothesized that among program mothers

> this style arose from their earlier interactions with the day-care staff, interactions that developed an expectation that there should be information exchange between parents and the institutions caring for their children. That they have continued this practice so many years after the program ended also suggests that they feel competent to deal with whatever information such exchanges reveal. (pp. 388–389)

By design, Head Start provides opportunities for parents to develop their skills in community organizing and decision making within an institutional setting. The local Head Start Parent Advisory Committee is a major avenue for such skill-building. The consequences of these Head Start activities are not clear. The Head Start literature contains a good amount of positive anecdotal information about the relation of Head Start activities to changes in institutions in the community, but lacks well-designed studies on the processes and effects of parent participation in community institutions. Two limitations of the existing research are especially problematic. One is that studies of Head Start impact on the community generally have not been clear about the role and relative impact of various Head Start change agents. For example, is change in a local institution (e.g., greater receptivity of local schools to parent involvement) a function of Head Start staff, parents, and/or the Head Start program as a prototype service? Further, Head Start's influence on institutional change cannot be separated from larger societal forces such as the Civil Rights Movement operating at the time the community impact studies were undertaken (Stearns, 1971). A second major limitation is that the design of existing research does not permit a determination of the causal relationship between Head Start participation and parental involvement in the community. One study found that most parents who were involved in Head Start and subsequently in other community organizations were involved in their communities prior to their Head Start affiliation (Midco Educational Associations, 1972).

Among the more interesting findings of an extensive study of Head Start's community impact is that Head Start centers with high parent participation were more active in affecting institutional change in the community than Head Start centers where parent participation was low (Midco, 1972). The study also found that in centers where parents were not highly involved in Head Start, parents expressed less confidence in their ability to influence their local school system. Among the antecdotal reports in the literature are numerous illustrations of Head Start parents having direct impact on medical services (e.g., increased availability of services to low-income families, see Midco, 1972) and public school systems (e.g., greater use of aides in classrooms, see *Head Start Assessment,* 1977).

It was noted earlier in this chapter that an anticipated outcome of parent participation in early childhood programs is improved quality of child care programs because parents possess knowledge about child care programs that strengthens their role as informed consumers of child care services. Apparently, no research has been carried out on·this possibility.

Program resources

The existing literature contains many anecdotal reports of how parent participation in early childhood programs serves to strengthen program resources. In most reported instances, parents have functioned as lobbyists in efforts to secure additional resources for program operations from public and private sources. The reports represent publicly funded early childhood centers serving racially diverse populations (Joffe, 1977), a child care center serving low-income families (Midco, 1972), the National Head Start Association, which actively lobbies for the Head Start program at the national level (O'Keefe, 1979), and the federal Follow Through program (Olmsted & Rubin, 1983). In the Follow Through program, for instance, parents have played a major role in securing or restoring legislative support during several funding crises in the program's history (Olmsted & Rubin, 1983). These reports are understandably unclear about the level of resources programs would have secured without parent lobbying activities. Parent participation as program volunteers also is a resource for early childhood programs. There is limited systematic literature on the effects of this role, although anecdotal reports point to positive impact on program responsiveness as well as on parental self-esteem (Robinson & Choper, 1979).

Summary

The participation of low-income parents in early childhood programs has been found to be associated with increased levels of formal education, positive attitudes toward self, and active involvement in other institutions in the community. It is unclear whether program participation is a causal factor in these outcomes. Most of the studies have designs that do not permit causal statements, and at least one study found that parents who were active in an early childhood program and subsequently in other community institutions had active community involvements prior to participation in the early childhood program. The literature on this topic contains abundant anecdotal reports of positive changes in adult functioning and in community institutions as a result of parent participation in early childhood programs.

Conclusions

The studies reviewed in this chapter contribute in important ways to our understanding of relations between parents and staff in early childhood settings. At the same time, *the existing research is limited in the questions examined and in the methodologies employed.* There are major gaps in the current research knowledge, and existing data sets largely have been generated through cross-sectional research designs employing self-report interview and questionnaire methods. Little can be said about causal relations or changes over time. The absence of observational data and longitudinal studies is particularly striking. Data from several of the major studies were collected more than a decade ago.

The current state of research limits the field's ability to set forth an empirically derived set of standards for interactions between families and early childhood programs. However, it would be inappropriate to conclude that, in the absence of data, relations between families and programs are unimportant. There are strong philosophical (see Chapter 1) and theoretical (see Chapter 2) arguments for fostering close ties between parents and early childhood settings.

The existing research points to *marked variations between and within early childhood settings regarding levels of program-parent interaction.* There are significant differences across programs in the frequency of parent participation in various operations, and in the nature of interpersonal ties between parents and staff. Among child care centers, there are considerable differences in the provision of parent- and family-oriented support services. Within-center variations in levels of program-parent interaction are underscored by findings from a variety of settings that indicate major differences across parents in program participation rates. This conclusion limits generalizations about levels of parent-staff interaction and suggests that for many programs a major challenge is to extend parental participation beyond a small cadre of highly involved parents.

Assessments of the current quality of relations between parents and early childhood programs require clear expectations of what the relationship should be like. Descriptive information on the characteristics of program-parent relations is of little use without a set of practice guidelines for determining the extent to which the current state of affairs satisfies desired standards. Comparisons of reality with preferred or ideal conditions are hampered by the relatively small number of existing studies and by the limited number of operational definitions and standards regarding desired parent-staff interactions. For instance, available research data address only several of the NAEYC criteria for parent-staff interaction (see Chapter 1).

If current practice guidelines (see Chapter 1) and theoretical propositions about inter-setting relations (see Chapter 2) are applied to the existing research knowledge, it would appear that *in general the existing quality of relations between parents and staff in center-based early childhood programs does not satisfy recommendations for appropriate program-family interconnections advanced by leaders in the field.* Less is known about parent-provider relations in family day care, but the available data suggest that interactions between parents and family child care providers may more closely approximate desired practices than parent-staff exchanges in center programs. The above generalization is offered with the understanding that, as noted above, there is considerable variability within and across programs.

While a majority of parents and caregivers has been found to communicate in person on a weekly or more frequent basis, the exchange typically occurs at drop-off and pickup times, when individuals may be preoccupied with other matters. Also, for late afternoon or evening retrievals, the child care staff on duty may not have been with the child all day and therefore may have limited information on the child's day. Perhaps these factors contribute to the high level of parent and caregiver dissatisfaction with discussion of activities at the center. The available data also suggest that the information flow has a tendency to be one-way, from center to parent. The guideline of parental involvement in curriculum and program policy decisions suggested by the National Black Child Development Institute, which long has been a performance standard in Head Start, appears to be in practice in only a minority of child care centers. Further, the traditional home-school linkage modes of parent-teacher conferences and staff visits to the home seem to be infrequently employed in child care centers.

Overall, the parent-staff relationship appears to be more of a problem for early childhood staff than for parents. Several studies indicate that caregivers are considerably more dissatisfied than parents with the level of parent-staff communication, even when parents have limited contact with staff. Early childhood staff and parents also seem to differ in the types of information each group sees as appropriate to discuss within the parent-staff relationship. It would appear, then, that caregiver images of the desired program-family relationship differ from prevailing parental images.

The image of parent education as an expert telling a group of mothers about the ages and stages of child development is neither complete nor accurate as a portrayal of many of today's programs.

Chapter 4

Parent education and support: Program processes and effects

EFFORTS TO ENHANCE the childrearing competence of families are not new (Brim, 1959). A view of parents as the child's "first and foremost teacher" has dominated social reform movements with regularity since the publication of an infant education handbook by John Amos Comenius (1592–1670) (see Fein, 1980). In the past three decades, the primacy of the family has commanded considerable attention in attempts to design effective early childhood intervention programs and, more recently, in efforts to respond to the dramatic changes in family structure and traditional support systems for parents. Chapter 1 identified some of the recent developments.

Significant diversity in program ideologies and approaches has resulted from the past 25 years of experimentation with programs to support and inform parents with young children. The image of parent education as an expert telling a group of mothers about the ages and stages of child development is neither complete nor accurate as a portrayal of many of today's programs. Consider the following contrasts: Some programs focus on family-community relations while others teach parents how to stimulate a child's cognitive development. Some programs prescribe specific skills and styles in relating to young children while other programs encourage parents to become informed decision makers in the use of child development information. Some programs are designed primarily to disseminate child development information to parents while others attempt to foster supportive relationships among program participants. Some programs are highly structured while others pursue content of interest to the parent participants. In some programs the staff serve as child development experts while other programs adhere to a self-help model with staff in nondirective facilitator roles. There also are important differences in the use of professionals, assistants or volunteers, program length (weeks versus years), and program setting (group- versus home-based).

*A view of parents as the child's "first and foremost teacher"
has dominated social reform movements with regularity
since the publication of an infant education handbook by
John Amos Comenius (1592–1670).*

This chapter reviews findings of selected research on programs that seek to improve the family's childrearing capacity by providing information and social support. It is organized into the following three major sections: a description of emerging directions in the field; a summary of several studies of program processes in group- and home-based delivery strategies; and a review of research on program effects.

Emerging directions

In the past decade, there have been major changes in the ideological framework, content, and procedures of programs aimed at parents. The emerging directions include (1) an interest in matching programs and parent populations; (2) a movement toward a realignment of relations between program staff and participants; and (3) increasing programmatic attention to the social context of parent functioning. See Powell (1988a) for an overview of these trends and Powell (1988b) for in-depth treatment of each.

Efforts to match program design to the characteristics of specific parent populations reflect an interest in individual differences in parents' needs, characteristics, and program participation patterns. The notion that a particular program model can work with *any* parent has given way to questions about matching parents to different types of programs. One indication of this shift is the movement from standardized to individualized programs. Increasingly, programs attempt to tailor services and methods to the perceived and expressed needs of participants, especially those living in low-income or high-risk circumstances. Interest in matching programs to parents also is evident in current efforts to develop programs that are responsive to cultural characteristics and values of ethnic populations. The field has moved beyond the notion that, to serve ethnic minority populations, the primary task is to make existing programs accessible to members of ethnic minorities. There is recognition that programs also need to be culturally responsive (Rogler, Malgady, Costantino, & Blumenthal, 1987).

Lessons from experiences with early intervention programs in the 1960s and 1970s are responsible for the increased interest in program-parent congruence (see Powell, 1988a). One lesson surrounded the problems encountered in the use of group discussion methods with low-income populations (Chilman, 1973). This was one of the earliest signs that parent education methods frequently used with middle-class populations might not readily transfer to low-income parents. Although factors other than (or

Efforts to match program design to the characteristics of specific parent populations reflect an interest in individual differences in parents' needs, characteristics, and program participation patterns.

in addition) to the group format may have been responsible for the limited appeal of group-based interventions with low-income populations, the group approach was targeted as the source of difficulty, giving rise to the idea that home-based strategies are superior methods for reaching the hard-to-reach.

Another lesson stems from large-scale efforts to replicate intervention programs in diverse communities. Planned variation studies involving Head Start and Follow Through models pointed to the impossibility of exactly duplicating a program model in different communities. The lesson learned was that the effects of model programs depend in part on a program's interactions with local circumstances in the host community (Halpern & Larner, 1988).

The roles of professionals and other staff in parent programs constitute a topic of great interest in the field today (Powell, 1984a). A review of the program literature suggests a trend toward collaborative, equal relations between parents and program staff wherein the flow of influence is reciprocal. The concept of parental *empowerment* reflects this shift (Cochran, 1988a). The terms *client* and *expert* have come to represent an outdated paradigm of professional dominance and parental passivity as program participants. Increasingly, there are indications of program staff serving as facilitator of goals and activities jointly determined by parents and staff; in one variant of this trend, the program role is to provide child development information so parents can make informed decisions about childrearing approaches.

Current interest in altering the traditional balance of power in parent-professional relations stems from the social and political currents of the Civil Rights Movement and Great Society programs of the 1960s (see Powell, 1988b). Specifically, the sources of influence on this trend include the following: (a) criticisms of the deficit model inherent in the first round of early intervention programs, where often it was assumed that targeted families provided deficient childrearing environments; (b) the provisions for parent participation mandated in social and educational program legislation (i.e., the "maximum feasible participation" principle of the Economic Opportunity Act of 1964); (c) societal concerns about professional involvement in the private matters of family childrearing (Lasch, 1977); and (d) adoption of the idea that adult change processes involve active roles in program participation (see Chapter 1).

The third emerging direction in the field of parent programs today is the interest in programs that enhance the social context of parenthood. Efforts are being made to strengthen parents' social networks, social support, and community ties as a buffer against stressful life circumstances and transi-

The effects of model programs depend in part on a program's interactions with local circumstances in the host community.

Widespread concern about the viability of conventional support systems for families with young children has led to the argument that parent support programs can be a modern-day version of the traditional extended family.

There is a trend toward collaborative, equal relations between parents and program staff wherein the flow of influence is reciprocal.

tions. Interest in the socioecological influences on human development is reflected in use of the term *parent support* in lieu of or in addition to the more conventional *parent education* label to describe programs for parents. This name change represents a substantive shift in program assumptions about the determinants of parent functioning. The traditional parent education program assumes the dissemination of information to parents will affect behaviors and attitudes, whereas the parent support approach assumes the provision of social support will positively influence parent functioning (for further discussion of this distinction, see Powell, 1988d). The interest in the social context of individual and family functioning is not unique to parent programs; equally strong movement in this direction can be found in the fields of public health, social work, and medicine.

Public policy analyses and research on the contexts of parenting have contributed to this growing interest in programs targeted at the ecology of family childrearing. The report of the Carnegie Council on Children (Keniston & the Carnegie Council on Children, 1977) underscored the economic and social stresses on families. The theoretical and empirical work of Urie Bronfenbrenner (1974, 1978, 1979) has been profoundly influential in stimulating this shift in the field of parent education. Of special significance was Bronfenbrenner's (1974) report on the effects of early childhood intervention, in which he argued that parents need ecological intervention in the form of family support systems. Demographic changes also have contributed significantly to the field's interest in the social context of parenthood. As described in Chapter 1, widespread concern about the viability of conventional support systems for families with young children has led to the argument that parent support programs can be a modern-day version of the traditional extended family (Slaughter, 1983; Weissbourd, 1987).

Life in programs: Process studies

Most evaluations of parent education and support programs have been designed to assess outcomes, with little investigation of the ways in which programs function or how parents differ in their program participation. The prevailing intent has been to determine whether there is any proof of a program's effectiveness rather than to illuminate program processes. Outcome studies are a needed and highly useful line of research. However, outcome research generally does not provide data that help program designers make decisions about the kinds of strategies that will work with different types of parents. For this we need research on program processes.

Traditional parent education programs assume the dis-semination of information to parents will affect behaviors and attitudes; the parent support approach assumes the provision of social support will positively influence parent functioning.

Discussion groups*

What goes on in parent discussion groups? This question was a focus of research carried out on the Child and Family Neighborhood Program (CFNP), an experimental parent-child educational support program established in 1978 by the Merrill-Palmer Institute in cooperation with the Wayne-Westland Community Schools in Michigan (Powell, 1987c). The program was in a low-income, suburban Detroit neighborhood. Parents (mostly mothers) were recruited for participation when their babies were under 6 months of age. Long-term participation (two years) was encouraged.

The core of the program was a small, long-term discussion group of 5 to 10 mothers who met twice weekly for two hours. Paraprofessionals trained in child development and group processes took responsibility for the meetings, most of which were characterized by brief staff presentations and considerable discussion among participants. The group used no determined set of topics or structured curriculum; rather, discussions focused on topics of interest to group members.

The program was housed in a duplex renovated for program purposes. Children accompanied parents to the program, and a preschool was located on the premises for older siblings. Individual consultations were available through home visits for parents desiring staff involvement in social service or medical issues. A public health nurse and community outreach worker carried out most of these individual sessions.

The value of "kitchen talk." One of the areas of interest in this process study was the nature of conversations during formal versus informal program time (see Powell & Eisenstadt, 1988). Most group- or center-based programs include a break time that provides an informal setting for conversations without staff guidance or involvement. In the CFNP, much of the informal break time was spent in the kitchen, with mothers standing or sitting around a large table. In contrast, the formal meeting segments occurred in a living room, with chairs arranged in a large circle.

Over a 12-month period, there was a steady expansion of break time and a corresponding decrease in the formal meeting time. For example, in the first quarter an average of 18 minutes was spent in the midsession break and an average of 58 minutes in the formal meeting. By the third quarter, an average of 29 minutes was spent in the break and an average of 44

---

* This section is adapted from: Douglas R. Powell. (1987). Life in a parent support program: Research perspectives. *Family Resource Coalition Report, 6*(3), 4–5, 18.

Parent discussion groups need to include both adequate time and comfortable physical surroundings for informal conversations controlled by parents.

minutes in the formal meeting. It appeared that mothers desired the informal "kitchen talk."

Given this pattern, an important question is whether the informal interaction in the kitchen played a positive role in the program. If a goal of a parent program is to provide individuals with new insight and ideas about children and parenthood, then it is useful to know whether the informal exchange of ideas among peers simply reinforces the status quo among peers or offers perspectives that extend and perhaps challenge existing knowledge and beliefs.

Structured observations of 101 group sessions were conducted for one year (see Powell & Eisenstadt, 1988). The findings suggest that the informal "kitchen talk" was not wasted time. It was as stimulating as staff-directed conversations in the formal setting. Nonroutine conversation — that is, exploration of a topic in detail and/or in an atypical manner — occurred in 55% of the discussion sequences in the formal setting, and in 49% of discussion sequences in the informal kitchen setting. Further, the informal "kitchen talk" was a complement to the more formal group discussions; conversations about individual babies occurred with greater frequency in the informal setting than in the formal setting.

We cannot assume the frequency or content of nonroutine conversations in the informal setting would have occurred without the staff-directed formal meeting segment. Discussions in the formal meeting may have been a stimulus for conversations during the kitchen break time. It does appear, however, that the informal conversations were an important element of the group's experience. It seems worthwhile, then, for parent discussion groups to permit both adequate time and comfortable physical surroundings for informal conversations controlled by parents.

Social context of parenthood. The structured observations of 101 group sessions over a one-year period uncovered another pattern: discussion of parent-child topics declined in both the formal and informal settings over time. Discussion of child and parenting decreased from 44% in the first quarter to 18% in the fourth quarter in the formal setting; there was a similar decrease in the informal setting.

What replaced the decreasing discussion of parent-child topics? Conversations about the larger social environment — extended family, marital relations, careers, jobs, neighborhood, crime, community services, housing, and the like — increased in both the formal and informal settings. Discussion of topics related to self (e.g., birth control, weight control, hobbies) also increased, as did topics related to the business of the parent groups.

Discussion of parent-child topics declines in both formal and informal program settings over time. Conversations about the larger social environment — extended family, marital relations, careers, jobs, neighborhood, crime, community services, housing, and the like — increase in both settings.

It is common for parents to indicate that a major benefit of program involvement is "learning that others are having experiences similar to mine."

The role of social comparison. Experienced workers in parent group programs are aware that the opportunity for social comparison is a key reason parents join and participate in group sessions. It is common for parents to indicate that a major benefit of program involvement is "learning that others are having experiences similar to mine." Research on the CFNP pointed to an unanticipated "outcome" of this type of verbal behavior in a group meeting.

In the longitudinal examination of patterns of program participation, it was discovered that reporting personal experiences — what the investigators labeled *narrative behavior* — was significantly related to subsequent feelings of closeness to group members (see Eisenstadt & Powell, 1987). Specifically, participants who described their experiences with childrearing and parenthood in the initial months of group life were more likely to report a sense of being well-connected to other group members by six months of group involvement. Hence, these data provide empirical support for the program practice of encouraging parents to report their experiences with parenting tasks and issues. One "outcome" of such discussions seems to be the development of supportive ties with peers.

Home visiting programs

Home visiting programs represent an important strategy of parent-focused early education. In the past decade, educational, health, and mental health agencies have implemented scores of programs. Some programs are staffed by lay persons (Larner & Halpern, 1987); others use professionals. Target populations often are young, low income, geographically and/or socially isolated, and, in some cases, members of ethnic minority populations (Halpern, 1984). Home visiting programs represent somewhat of a "black box" in that little research has been carried out that describes what happens in the privacy of the family domain (Larner, Nagy, & Halpern, 1987).

A recent national study of the home-based option in Head Start provides information on the nature of home visits in an educational program aimed at low-income families with young children (Meleen, Love, & Nauta, 1988). In 1986–87, when the study was conducted, 451 Head Start programs were serving some 30,339 children through a home-based approach. The Meleen et al. study collected program service data on 95% of these programs and conducted observations and interviews at eight selected sites. The information reported below comes from observations of four home visits at each of the eight sites. The observed home visits lasted an average of 75 minutes. All eight programs used some form of curriculum or lesson plan for the visits.

The findings of the Meleen et al. (1988) study may be summarized as follows. An important focus of the home visit was helping parents to become more effective educators of their own children. One-third of the 75-minute session was spent working with parents; only a small segment of the visit was devoted exclusively to the child. The study reports that parents spent almost one-half of the home visit time practicing activities with the home visitor and/or the child. The visits had a predominantly educational focus; only a small portion of time was devoted to social service needs. Home visitors assigned parents activities to carry out with their child between home visits and followed up on what had been done. It appeared that home visitors tailored activities to meet the specific needs of parent and child. Some specific details of these findings are discussed below.

A crucial question for home-based programs involving both parent and child is the relative amount of time in the home visit focused on the child versus the parent versus the parent-child dyad. Across the eight programs, an average of 16 minutes of the 75-minute visit was devoted to activities with the parent as the primary focus. Activities designed for both parent and child occupied an average of 12 minutes. About 63% of the home visit time was focused on the child, with parents reportedly taking an active role. The home visitor spent almost half of the 16 minutes devoted to parent-focused activities giving the parent information about teaching strategies, stages of child development, and the purpose of a specific home visit activity. Some of the parent-focused activities also included assessing child needs and planning future home visit activities. There also were discussions about parenting and child discipline, and the home visitors gave parents hints on how to deal with specific problems. An average of five minutes was devoted to giving specific assignments for parents to work on between home visits, with home visitor follow-up on the assignments at subsequent visits.

A small portion (4 minutes) of the observed home visit time had a social service orientation. Topics discussed ranged from parental interest in adult education, job training, or employment to issues related to a pending divorce, child custody, and free legal assistance. There also were discussions about needs for financial aid and furniture, how to apply for reduced-price lunches and loans, illnesses or deaths in the family, and food programs. Parents were reminded of the child's medical examination and immunization needs. In four of the eight sites there was considerable emphasis on nutrition.

Of the two-thirds of the home visit time devoted to activities focused on the child, major emphasis was given to child development, education, and school readiness issues. Across the eight sites, an average of 21 minutes was

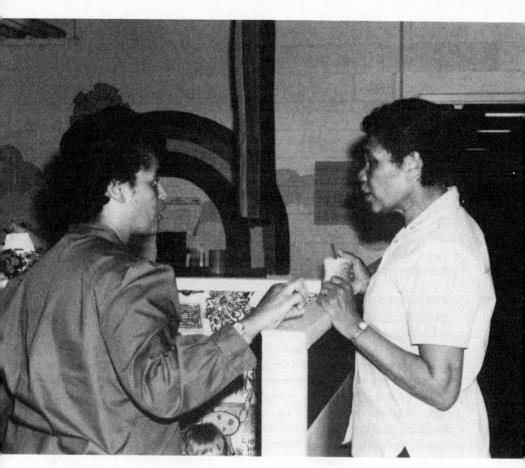

The Head Start home visiting component focuses on child development and education; home visits operated by health or mental health agencies might have more of a social service orientation.

spent teaching or practicing traditional readiness or basic skills, such as mastering shapes, colors, numbers, concepts, matching, letter recognition, and the like. Activities designed to develop the child's fine and gross motor skills occupied about 8 minutes of home visit time on the average. Siblings of the enrolled child frequently were involved in child activities if close in age. The home visitor either worked with two children at the same time or alternated with the parent.

The Head Start home visiting component has a distinctly educational focus. It seems probable that a different set of patterns would emerge in descriptive research on home visits operated by health or mental health agencies.

Variations in parent participation

Observers of parent programs have long recognized that there are considerable differences among parents in terms of their program participation patterns and what they gain from a program. Recently several researchers have investigated these individual differences. Information about the ways in which parents respond to a program may explain program effects with greater power and precision, and might be used to design programs that respond to parents' needs and characteristics.

Research has found important differences in how parents participate in a program. Some parents may relate mostly to the staff, other parents may focus most of their program time on other parents (Powell, 1985). Some may make a substantial contribution to group discussions while others do not (Eisenstadt & Powell, 1987). Some mothers more readily accept the ideas and activities the program offers (Lambie, Bond, & Weikart, 1974).

Studies suggest that personality factors may influence parents' participation in a program. For example, the parent's disposition to be expressive or controlled when dealing with impulses was found to be a reliable predictor of participation in a parent-child educational support program for low-income mothers. Expressive mothers were significantly more likely to contribute verbally to group discussions and to form friendships with other program participants (Eisenstadt & Powell, 1987).

The Child and Family Resource Program was most successful with mothers who felt confident about their ability to control events in their environments. These mothers were more likely to enroll in school or job training, experienced less difficulty in obtaining health services, and were more flexible in their attitudes toward childrearing (Travers, Nauta, & Irwin, 1982).

Environmental conditions also may influence program participation. Mothers with extensive family and friendship ties have been found to be

Most parent programs have high dropout rates. A major task for planners is to develop programs that respond to parents' needs.

---

more responsive to home-based parent educators (Kessen, Fein, Clarke-Stewart, & Starr, 1975) and more likely to form friendships with other parents in the program (Powell, 1983) than mothers with fewer social ties. Cochran and Henderson (1985) found that program effects varied in relation to ethnicity and family structure.

In a longitudinal study of participation in the CFNP described earlier in this chapter, mothers who were experiencing a high level of environmental stress attended program sessions less often, were in the group for a longer time before they contributed to group discussions, and needed more time to form friendships with other mothers than did mothers experiencing lower levels of environmental stress (Eisenstadt & Powell, 1987).

More research is needed to develop a clearer understanding of what types of parents gain the most and the least from what types of programs. The available findings suggest that program designers need to be sensitive to the hidden prerequisites (e.g., social skills) necessary for productive program participation (e.g., contributing to group discussion). A major task for program planners is to develop programs that respond to parents' needs. At the same time, program designers need to be cognizant of parents' personal characteristics and life conditions that are well beyond what can be changed or controlled by any social intervention. It may be unrealistic and even unproductive to expect parents to be ideal participants.

Finding ways to sustain program participation is a perennial concern for early childhood educators. While some programs seem to be more success-ful than others in keeping parent involved, most have a high dropout rate. For example, 48% of the participants in the Houston PCDC serving low-income parents left the program during a 2-year period (Johnson & Breckenridge, 1982). In a 9-week program aimed at a middle-class group, 41% of the parents did not complete the series (Lochman & Brown, 1980).

Two major reasons for high attrition rates are that families move and parents change employment frequently. Indications are that those who drop out of programs early tend to have fewer children (Lambie et al., 1974; Powell, 1984b) and a more limited network of friends and relatives (Powell, 1984b) than long-term participants.

Summary

Little process research has been carried out on family support and education programs, but the studies reviewed here suggest a view of programs as fluid, dynamic entities. Longitudinal research on discussion groups involving low-income mothers points to the importance of infor-mal exchanges during program time, parental interest in the conditions of parenthood, and the role of social comparison in fostering close interpersonal ties among program participants. A recent study of the home-based option in Head Start underscores the educational nature of the program and the parent's active role in the home visit session. Research conducted on both group- and home-based interventions suggests that variations in program participation are related to parents' dispositional tendencies, feelings of control over the environment, social networks, and level of environmental stress.

Program effects

The level of recent activity in developing programs aimed at families of young children far exceeds the amount of evaluation research that has been conducted. What we know empirically about the effects of parent education and support programs comes primarily from a small but impressive group of field-based studies of interventions using a true experimental design (e.g., Klaus & Gray, 1968; Lambie et al., 1974; Kessen et al., 1975; Dickie & Gerber, 1980; Gray & Ruttle, 1980; Andrews et al., 1982; Travers et al., 1982; Cochran & Henderson, 1985; Scarr & McCartney, 1988) or quasiexperimental design (e.g., Slaughter, 1983; Seitz, Rosenbaum, & Apfel, 1985; Lally, Mangione, & Honig, 1988). The extent of focus on the child versus the parent varies in these interventions; in some programs the parent was the primary or only client while in other programs there was direct work with the child (e.g., group experiences) in addition to services aimed at the parent.

Methodological considerations

The evaluation of community-based programs aimed at parents is fraught with difficulty. The design and methods of many parent-oriented programs conflict with the tenets of experimental design. Thus, laboratory research procedures require adaptations to the idiosyncratic world of parent programs; sometimes the compromises stretch experimental approaches beyond their limits. Therefore, evaluation results often lack power and precision, allowing only equivocal statements about program effects. Brief acknowledgment of these problems provides a framework for understanding the findings and limitations of existing outcome studies. For recent detailed discussions of methodological issues in family-oriented early intervention programs, interested readers are referred to Clarke-

Stewart and Apfel (1978), Gray and Wandersman (1980), Halpern (1984), Campbell (1987), Powell (1987a), Seitz (1987), and Weiss and Jacobs (1988).

The realities of program life have important implications for the design of program evaluations. One reality factor is the imprecise quality of the treatment variable. In interventions where workers tailor the services to meet the needs of individual parents or where programs actively encourage a range of participation modes, there is not a uniform delivery of the program across all participants. Degradation of the treatment variable also can occur even when an effort has been made to keep the content and contact frequency of program services constant across participants. As noted in the foregoing description of process research, there is evidence that participants can have diverse program experiences within a uniform program.

Until recently, it has been common for evaluations of parent programs to use a pre-post design with no control or comparison group. This weak evaluation approach contributes little to our understanding of program effects (for a critical review, see Clarke-Stewart & Apfel, 1978). While true experimental designs have been strongly recommended for studies of parent program outcomes (Reicken & Boruch, 1974; Scarr & McCartney, 1988), random assignment of participants to treatment and control groups often is not feasible in *ongoing* community-based parent programs. Moreover, random assignment does not prevent the problem of selective attrition of participants, resulting in nonequivalent control and experimental groups at the time of follow-up assessments. Recently investigators have used quasiexperimental designs, including treatment partitioning and time-lag designs (see Seitz, 1987). Well-implemented quasiexperimental designs have considerable potential but cannot be viewed as an equivalent substitute for a true experimental design. A case in point is the evaluation of the Mother-Child Home Program (see pp. 104–105). An evaluation employing an experimental design (Madden, O'Hara, & Levenstein, 1984) found less positive effects than an earlier study that used a quasiexperimental design (Madden, Levenstein, & Levenstein, 1976).

The selection and measurement of outcome variables constitute another problematic area of evaluation. The difficulties here include a lack of consensus in the field about appropriate outcomes of parent-oriented programs, and the limited number of reliable and valid measures of child and family functioning that are relevant to anticipated program outcomes. With regard to the field's measurement consensus problem, no set of outcome variables is commonly recognized as an appropriate indicator of program effectiveness. A key issue here is the extent to which child variables

Some argue that parent programs exist to improve child functioning, while others submit that the growth and development of adult participants as individuals and parents should be the primary focus.

should be used to assess the effects of a parent-oriented program. Some argue that parent programs exist to improve child functioning, while others submit that the growth and development of adult participants as individuals and parents should be the primary focus of outcome assessments (see Powell, 1987a).

Effects on children

Studies of parent education programs have found short-term effects on children. Children's IQ has been examined most frequently and has been found to increase as an apparent result of the parents' program participation (e.g., Lambie et al., 1974; Gray & Ruttle, 1980; Andrews et al., 1982; Slaughter, 1983). There also is some indication that parent programs have an influence on children's school performance (Cochran & Henderson, 1985).

While these immediate child effects point to a promising trend, not all programs have been found to be effective. A recent experimental evaluation of a widely used parent-focused early intervention program found no short-term effects on child or mother. Scarr and McCartney (1988) evaluated the Mother-Child Home Program (MCHP) developed by Phyllis Levenstein (1977, 1988) using a sample of 125 families with 24-month-olds representing a range of socioeconomic status in Bermuda. The MCHP uses home visits to demonstrate for mothers many ways to interact positively with their children and to provide more educational experiences for them. In the Scarr and McCartney evaluation, two-thirds of the families were randomly assigned to the program and one-third to a no-treatment control group. The program had few demonstrable effects on a broad range of 17 child measures of cognitive, social, and emotional outcomes, and on 43 measures of maternal behavior and attitudes. The investigators engaged in a diligent search for treatment interactions, but found that treatment effects were not concentrated in any one segment of the sample, including those of low socioeconomic status (see also McCartney & Scarr, 1989).

It is especially noteworthy when a well-designed evaluation fails to uncover positive effects of a prominent program in the parent-child intervention field. What might account for the results? Scarr and McCartney (1988) suggest that one reason for the lack of effects is that nearly all the children were in group child care due to maternal employment; thus, the children had preschool experiences comparable to those intended by the MCHP. Levenstein (1989) argues that because two-thirds of the families in the Scarr and McCartney evaluation were not socioeconomically disadvantaged, the results point to the "futility and even wastefulness" of using the MCHP to prevent educational disadvantage in children not at risk for such disadvantage. She suggests that parental motivation and level of education may be stronger predictors of school disadvantage than poverty alone, and argues that the lottery method employed in the Bermuda experiment attracted highly motivated parents. However, a reanalysis of the Scarr and McCartney data using maternal education as the criterion of disadvantage found that the MCHP was not effective for this population (McCartney & Scarr, 1989). (See Levenstein [1989] and McCartney and Scarr [1989] for discussion of this and other methodological issues raised by Levenstein regarding the Bermuda evaluation.)

The limited scope of the intervention also could have contributed to the lack of MCHP effects. Levenstein et al. (1983) intentionally kept the program "as simple as possible" (p. 238) yet a recent analysis of compensatory preschool programs (Ramey, Bryant, & Suarez, 1985) suggests a relationship between program intensity and outcome (see pp. 108–109). Questions also could be raised about limitations inherent in the MCHP approach; for instance, Cochran (1988b) has voiced concern that the MCHP "left too little room for validation of parental worth" (p. 74). However, Levenstein (1989) has indicated that sponsors of the MCHP replications have observed mental health benefits for parents and families, but apparently this has not been investigated systematically.

It is worthwhile to contrast the Scarr and McCartney finding of no effects with the evaluation results of the Parent Child Development Centers (PCDCs). Conceived by the U.S. Office of Economic Opportunity during the Great Society era — when considerable excitement and financial resources were available for tackling poverty through early childhood intervention — the PCDC enterprise was an ambitious and well-planned research and program development strategy (Dokecki, Hargrove, & Sandler, 1983). Programs were to be developed, stabilized, evaluated, and then replicated and evaluated in different sites. Leading scholars as well as the technical resources of preeminent institutions were tapped for the project.

Three original PCDC sites were established in New Orleans, Louisiana; Houston, Texas; and Birmingham, Alabama. Each offered comprehensive services to low-income families with young children. The curriculum for mothers included information on child development and childrearing practices, home management, nutrition and health, mothers' personal development, and government and community resources. There also was a simultaneous program for children and an extensive array of medical and social services for participating families. The plan called for mothers to remain in the program until their baby was 36 months of age. There were differences in this general model at the three sites, including the following:

Studies indicate that parent programs lead to only short-term gains in child IQ but may have long-term effects of decreasing negative behavior and use of special education classes.

the entry ages of children ranged from 2 months to New Orleans to 12 months in Houston; the length of the program and intensity of weekly participation varied; staffing patterns differed across sites; and teaching-learning formats varied for mothers and children. Although proponents of the PCDC model argued it was cost effective in relation to the alternative expenses of child care and job training, the intervention was expensive in comparison to costs of child care or Head Start.

The evaluation of the PCDCs found that children in each of the three sites achieved superior Stanford-Binet scores at the time of program graduation (when children were 36 months of age). There also were significant effects on several development measures for children in the Birmingham and New Orleans programs. Further, program mothers in each of the sites scored significantly higher than control group mothers on dimensions of positive maternal behavior at time of graduation. In all three sites, significant differences between program and control group mothers emerged on several maternal dimensions after 24 months of participation.

While the PCDCs and the MCHP clearly differ in comprehensiveness, they are similar in that both focused on the mother-child dyad in contrast to the family and community orientation that subsequently commanded attention in the parent intervention field (see "Emerging Directions," pp. 90–93). Also, the programs were evaluated at a point when they had had a reasonable time to develop and stabilize; thus, they met Campbell's (1987) criterion that only "proud programs" should be evaluated. Importantly, both the PCDC evaluation and the Scarr and McCartney evaluation of the MCHP employed experimental designs.

Do parent programs have long-term effects on children? It was found that the PCDC children maintained their IQ gains one year after leaving the program (Andrews et al., 1982) but not beyond (Bridgeman, Blumenthal, & Andrews, 1981). Further, of the few follow-up investigations conducted of other programs, there is no evidence to suggest that increases in child IQ are sustained more than one year after the end of participation in the program (Epstein & Weikart, 1979; Levenstein et al., 1983). These results regarding child IQ are similar to the findings of the follow-up studies of other preschool intervention projects (Lazar & Darlington, 1982). However, there are indications that children of parents involved in long-term parent education programs are less likely to be enrolled in special education classes as long as seven years after the program ends (Jester & Guinagh, 1983). Similar findings were uncovered for boys in a 10-year follow-up study of the Yale Child Welfare Project (Seitz et al.,

1985). Johnson and Breckenridge (1982) report in a 1- to 4-year follow-up study of the effects of the Houston Parent-Child Development Center that boys whose mothers did not participate in the program exhibited more negative behavior than boys whose mothers did participate. A 10-year follow-up study of the Syracuse Family Development Research Program found positive program effects on the incidence and severity of juvenile delinquency, child and parental attitudes toward self and the environment (i.e., problem-solving orientation), and school performance (grades, attendance, teacher ratings) of program girls but not boys in junior high school (Lally, Mangione, & Honig, 1988).

Effects on parents

Program effects on parents have not been studied as often as child effects. As noted above, in the PCDC evaluation there was evidence of immediate positive effects on maternal behavior (Andrews et al., 1982). Evaluations of other interventions have found positive effects on maternal use of positive and facilitative language interactions with the child (Lambie et al., 1974), open and flexible childrearing attitudes (Slaughter, 1983), and awareness of roles as educators (Travers et al., 1982). A study of a parent education/play group program found that participation increased fathers' sense of competence in parenting skills (McBride, 1988). Studies of popular parent education programs generally have examined changes in parental attitudes toward childrearing. A recent critique of 48 investigations of Parent Effectiveness Training, behavioral, and Adlerian programs found some changes in parental attitudes, but these changes were not always consistent and seemed to depend on the assessment tool (Dembo, Sweitzer, & Lauritzen, 1985). Methodological weaknesses also were found in many studies.

Consistent with the move toward family support programs, recent investigations have looked at program effects on the families' economic and life circumstances. Positive short- and long-term results have been found. In the Child and Family Resource Program, parents' feelings of control over their lives increased as a result of program participation (Travers et al., 1982). The Yale Child Welfare Project, an intensive program for impoverished mothers, still had an impact on family circumstances 10 years after the intervention ended. Mothers who had been in the Yale program were more likely to be self-supportive, have more education, and have smaller family sizes than mothers who had not been in the program (Seitz et al., 1985).

Identifying critical program attributes

Investigators have attempted to identify program elements that contribute to program effectiveness. Most of the effort has focused on the contributions of the program content and intensity (i.e., number of sessions and range of services) to the magnitude of program effects. This line of research has crucial implications for decisions about program design.

With regard to content, the available data do not provide convincing evidence that a particular type of child-related content is significantly more effective than another. A well-designed study that compared three curricula, each emphasizing a different aspect of development (social, language, and play), in a home-based program for mothers of toddlers found that the three curricula were equally powerful in influencing children's IQ (Kessen et al., 1975). Similarly, an across-program analysis of 28 different parent training programs found no relationship between the content of the curriculum and the degree of program impact on children's cognitive skills (Goodson & Hess, 1975).

Efforts to compare the effectiveness of popular parent education programs focused on child management skills have failed to identify a superior model. Comparisons of an Adlerian program to behavioral training (Frazier & Matthews, 1975) and Parent Effectiveness Training to behavioral training (Anchor & Thomason, 1977; Schofield, 1979; Pinsker & Geoffrey, 1981) did not identify one approach as more effective than another. Interestingly, Freeman (1975) found that an unstructured discussion group was just as effective as a highly structured Systematic Training for Effective Parenting (STEP) group in altering maternal attitudes.

There are suggestions in the literature that the specificity of training may be related to program outcomes. Based on a review of 18 preschool compensatory education programs, Ramey et al. (1985) suggested that global training about child development has little effect, but specific training stemming from a detailed curriculum can yield short-term changes in child and parent behavior. It is not known whether this suggestion would hold for middle-class parents. A parent training program that included lectures, discussion, and demonstration for 16 hours over 8 weeks to improve parental competence in predicting, eliciting, and responding to infant cues found positive effects on parental competence in reading infant cues and increased infant responsiveness to parent behavior (Dickie & Gerber, 1980). On the other hand, a study of a short-term parent group that emphasized support and education for new parents found no changes in the parents' sense of personal well-being or competence, or in the quality of interaction between spouses (Wandersman, Wandersman, & Kahn, 1980). Also, McGuire and Gottlieb (1979) report that a short-term support group for first-time parents had no impact on levels of stress, problem-solving knowledge, personal well-being, or health status, but 5 weeks after the last session the parents discussed childrearing matters with their friends, relatives, and acquaintances more often than parents who were not in the group.

There is evidence to suggest that the number of program contacts with a parent is related to program effects. In a review of outcome studies of 20 early intervention programs targeted at family functioning, Heinicke, Beckwith, and Thompson (1988) concluded that more pervasive and sustained effects are likely to be realized when the intervention includes 11 or more contacts over at least a three-month period. The investigators suggest that a certain duration of contact is needed to permit the development of a trusting relationship between the family and intervenor. The 20 interventions in the Heinicke et al. review were initiated sometime in the period from pregnancy to the first three months of the baby's life, included an articulated approach to changing some part of the family system (e.g., individual parents), and made systematic comparisons of the intervention group with either a control and/or contrast sample. The review included programs serving families with premature children, but excluded those with sick and/or handicapped children and children of physically and/or mentally ill parents.

Program intensity also can be measured by the comprehensiveness or range of services a program offers. Ramey et al. (1985) concluded that a child's intellectual development was improved most significantly when a high-quality child care program was offered in conjunction with other family services. Home visits alone have not been found to increase IQ by age 2, and home visits plus medical and educational intervention or parent-oriented training have moderate effects on IQ. This conclusion is based on a review of the 2-year results from 11 infancy intervention programs.

Seeking dimensions of program quality

The proliferation of parent education and support programs is likely to contribute pressure within and outside the field for a delineation of what constitutes a high-quality program. Although at present the field does not have a position statement on appropriate practices in parent-oriented programs, there is a growing body of empirical and theoretical work that can be used to identify program dimensions in need of attention in considerations about program quality. Four program dimensions are discussed below in the form of propositions (see Powell, 1988c).

An appropriate match of program and parent world views may be necessary to maintain program credibility in the eyes of parents, which may lead to better outcomes than if world views were mismatched.

First, it can be argued that in high-quality parent programs program content and methods appropriately match the needs and characteristics of individual parents. A major component of this dimension is that programs and parents share a similar world view of what parents need and want, and the means by which a program can best respond to parents. Examples of mismatches or dissimilar world views would be a program that wants parents to talk but a parent who wants to listen, or a program designed to teach infant stimulation exercises but a parent preoccupied with meeting basic survival needs. A mismatch of program and parent world views may undermine the credibility of a program in the eyes of parents. In the field of psychotherapy it has been suggested that outcomes are better when clients believe in their therapists and in the methods being employed.

Second, it can be argued that high-quality parent programs are characterized by collaborative relations between parents and program staff wherein there is shared decision-making control over the nature of parent participation. Collaborative ties can function as a structural mechanism for helping programs be sensitive and responsive to the needs and cultural norms of the population to be served, thereby assuring that a deficit model of program delivery will not prevail. Collaborative parent-staff relations reflect a theoretical view of adult change processes that suggest participation in democratic deliberations — formulating problems and negotiating solutions — influences the parent's relations with the child.

Third, the existing data can be interpreted as suggesting that parent programs need to maintain a balanced focus on the needs of both parent and child. As noted earlier in this chapter, there is a movement toward programs giving increased attention to the social contexts of parenthood. There are strong theoretical and empirical justifications for this movement, but at the same time there is the potential problem that parents' needs and interests may overshadow program attention to the child. Child issues may get lost in program attempts to tackle everyday and life event stressors. The literature on programs serving high-risk populations, for instance, points to the tendency for program workers to become heavily involved in crisis intervention surrounding pressing family matters (e.g., Halpern & Larner, 1988). There is some evidence to suggest that when parent-child programs serving low-income populations focus heavily on improving family situations and give minimal attention to child development issues, there may be no immediate positive effect on the child (Travers, Nauta, & Irwin, 1982).

*There are strong justifications for programs giving increased atten-
tion to the social context of parenthood, but care must be taken not to
let attention to the child's needs get lost in these efforts.*

Fourth, there is theoretical and some research support for using a significant amount of program time for open-ended parent discussion. Principles of adult education have long recommended that programs have a strong experiential component. This seems especially important in parent programs because parents are likely to process new information according to existing beliefs and constructs about their child and child development. Discussion provides an opportunity for parents to digest new insights in relation to existing ideas.

Summary

Major methodological problems in conducting outcome research on program effects include research accommodation of the realities of service delivery, evaluation design, and measurement problems. Only a handful of experimental evaluations have been carried out on parent-oriented early intervention programs. Most evaluations have found positive short-term effects on child and mother, and several studies have uncovered promising long-term effects on family variables but not on child IQ. Existing research on parent programs has failed to identify a superior curriculum content, but post-hoc analyses suggest that the number of program contacts and range of services offered to the family may be associated with the magnitude of program effects.

Chapter 5

Needed directions in research and program development

THE AIM OF THIS brief concluding chapter is to set forth some implications of the research reviewed in this monograph for future directions in research and program development. Many questions have been answered in this monograph, but often the answers lead to new questions. Many other questions have not been addressed, largely because data are not available. The directions suggested in this chapter are arbitrary and certainly not conclusive of the number of potentially productive domains of investigation explicitly or implicitly noted in the preceding pages.

Relations between families and early childhood programs

Fortunately, there is growing research activity aimed at identifying the characteristics of a high-quality early childhood environment (e.g., Phillips, 1987) and professional activity aimed at improving the conditions and characteristics of programs for young children. As shown in Chapter 2, the existing data on children's experiences with program-family discontinuity are too few and too inconclusive to offer *specific* guidance on what the parent-staff relationship should be like in a high-quality program. Many of the existing theoretical propositions as well as recommended practices have not been tested. Hence, there is a need to conduct field-based studies and experiments regarding the effects of the program-family relationship on children and families.

A first step toward this end is to clarify the image of how programs should relate to families. Is child care to be a service industry, with parents seen as customers to be pleased? Alternatively, are programs to be viewed as a modern-day version of the extended family, as leaders in the field have suggested? If so, how might a program put this image into operation? Is the program to be an extension of the home or of the elementary school? Answers to these questions have far-reaching implications for the roles and boundaries of the program-family intersection.

Few child care programs have taken steps to enable parental influence on program operations via parental review of budgets, curriculum, and staffing decisions. Research is needed on whether parent participation in program decision making contributes to increased program adaptiveness, or whether participation is implemented in a way that simply legitimizes the status quo.

Is child care to be seen as a service industry, with parents seen as customers to be pleased, or as a modern-day version of the extended family? Is the program to be an extension of the home or of the elementary school?

The bidirectional flow of information and influence in the program-family relationship is in need of attention at several levels. At an organizational level, the data reviewed in this monograph indicate that few child care programs have taken steps to enable parental influence on program operations via parental review of budgets, curriculum, and staffing decisions. More needs to be known about program responsiveness in settings where structural mechanisms exist and do not exist for parents to influence key program decisions. Does parent participation in program decision making contribute to increased program adaptiveness, or is participation implemented in a way that simply legitimizes the status quo (see Powell, in press; Beattie, 1985)? Organizational strategies for enabling program influence on parents' child development knowledge and childrearing practices traditionally include parent education meetings and parents serving as classroom volunteers in order to see teachers "model" appropriate behaviors with children. Because, increasingly, parents are less available for these types of activities (see Chapter 1), there is a need to experiment with alternative strategies. A hint of how to proceed may be found in Epstein's (1986) research on elementary school parents. Epstein found that teacher practices of requesting parents to help with children's learning activities *at home* had more dramatic positive links to parents' reactions to the school and on parent evaluations of the teacher than parent assistance at the school or general school-to-home communication.

Personal exchanges between parents and staff represent a second level through which programs and families can exert influence on one another. Because existing data suggest that much of the contact occurs within this context (see Chapter 3), it is a potentially fertile area for research. Basic questions remain unanswered: How do staff solicit, interpret, and respond to parental messages about program, child, and family? What are parents' interpretations of and responses to staff comments about child, program, and family? The personal level of information exchange also deserves attention in experimental strategies to improve program-family relations. Manipulation of variables such as staffing patterns and physical arrangements during child drop-off and pickup times may contribute to improved parent-staff communication. Maximizing program information gathering during the drop-off time seems especially important if a program is to respond adequately to situational or daily specifics regarding a child's functioning or family circumstance. Because data indicate that a sizable minority of parents do not enter the premises during the child drop-off time (see Chapter 3), a beginning point may be to alter policies and practices that minimize parental input during this daily transition for the child.

Parents are new to the executive task of coordinating the various socialization agencies in their child's life and are likely to need skills and information on how best to manage the relationship.

According to research, requesting parents to help with elementary school children's learning activities at home has more positive links to parents' reactions to the school and on parent evaluations of the teacher than parent assistance at the school or general school-to-home communications.

*It is important for training aimed at parents and teachers
to be respectful of their respective roles and to assume
mutuality or an equal power balance in the relationship.*

Training on how to facilitate program-family relations is needed for both program staff and parents. The content of most professional preparation programs for early childhood educators focuses on children, not adults, and the principles of effective practices with young children do not transfer to adults. As discussed in Chapter 3, early childhood staff have expressed more dissatisfaction than parents with the parent-teacher relationship, and thus teachers may be more likely to pursue specialized work on the topic. Parents should be integral to a training effort, however. They are new to the executive task of coordinating the various socialization agencies in their child's life (Keniston & Carnegie Council on Children, 1977) and are likely to need skills and information on how best to manage the relationship. Information on such topics as how to handle the child's transition into a new setting may be needed. For example, in a British study nearly one-half (47%) of mothers believed it was best for their child if the parent left immediately upon arrival at the nursery school instead of staying while the child settled in (Blatchford, Battle, & Mays, 1982); as discussed in Chapter 2, research indicates the latter practice is associated with the child's ease of adjustment to the center. It is important for training aimed at parents and teachers to be respectful of their respective roles and to assume mutuality or an equal power balance in the relationship.

While there appear to be few models of training for the parent-staff relations in early childhood settings, there are models at the elementary school level. One is the Cooperative Communication Between Home and School Project developed by the Family Matters program at Cornell University (Deann, 1983). The program is designed to strengthen skills in empathy building, creative problem solving, effective use of parent-teacher conferences and report cards, and conflict resolution. The program includes a six-week workshop series for parents, an in-service education program for elementary school teachers, and a monograph for school administrators. Program models that focus on parental involvement in the child's at-home learning also are available at the elementary school level. For example, the Home and School Institute based in Washington, D.C., has generated several special projects that foster parent-teacher partnerships surrounding elementary school children's learning activities in the home (Rich, 1985).

The need to address program-family relations is particularly acute for programs serving children who represent ethnic minorities and/or whose parents have limited formal education. Program-family discontinuity is significantly greater for these children and has been identified as a major cause of academic failure among ethnic minorities and other populations

Parents need to know what teachers regard as necessary preparation and experiences for school, and schools need to find culturally appropriate ways to deliver (not dilute) the curriculum.

Reseachers need a means of distinguishing among many theoretically and methodologically diverse family support and education programs.

---

in which parents have relatively few years of schooling (see Chapter 2). One of the proposals for addressing this problem is to implement what Laosa (1982) calls *articulated continuity* between the two environments (see Chapter 1).

How might continuity be achieved? In Chapter 2, I proposed that intersetting continuity consists of linkages (i.e., communication) and congruence (i.e., similarity of childrearing practices). For early childhood programs serving ethnic minorities, it seems that linkage strategies alone may prove to be inadequate in reducing the level of between-system discontinuity. Congruence needs to be addressed, and the method for doing so is of some debate in the field today. Should ethnic minority families be encouraged to modify their ways so there is greater compatibility with the school? Should the school change? Fillmore (1988) suggests the answer is "yes" to both of these questions. She argues that parents need to know what teachers regard as necessary preparation and experiences for school and that schools need to find culturally appropriate ways to deliver (not dilute) the curriculum. An example is the Kamehameha Early Education Program in Hawaii, which altered classroom practices but not goals on the basis of extensive study of Hawaiian cultural patterns (Tharp & Gallimore, 1988).

Parent education and support

Unlike the concern about relations between families and early childhood programs, program development activity aimed at enhancing family childrearing competence has not been limited. Weiss (1988) has characterized the family support and education field as a set of two dozen or so flagship research and demonstration programs and a larger fleet of small, grassroots community-based programs. As discussed in Chapter 4, the differences across programs with regard to theoretical and procedural approaches are significant.

The diversity in programming leads to a need for a classificatory system that helps the field as well as policymakers understand the conceptual and methodological distinctions among various programs. Until a useful taxonomy is available, advances in research and program development are likely to be hampered by the presumption of homogeneity across programs when in fact major theoretical and methodological diversification exists.

It is not clear whether parent-focused programs are more significant than programs that work primarily or exclusively with the child.

The need for research on family support and education programs cannot be overstated. Basic descriptive data of a national scope are needed on program services in relation to different types of families. Key program delivery problems such as how to reach hard-to-reach populations require thoughtful inquiry. In addition, considerably more needs to be known about program effects, especially on parent functioning and family variables. Attention also needs to be given to the program-family matches in relation to outcome. The field's growing interest in matching program structure and content to parents' needs and characteristics (see Chapter 4) cannot be pursued on empirical grounds without investigation of outcomes in relation to participant and program variables.

Additional research is needed on the short-term and long-term effects of parent programs in comparison to child-oriented programs. It is not clear that parent-focused programs are significantly more effective than programs that work primarily or exclusively with the child (Clark-Stewart & Fein, 1983). This unresolved question is one of the major policy issues in the field today (Zigler & Berman, 1983). Studies of program effects also are needed on parent support (versus education) programs and on program models involving middle-class families.

Future research also should focus more attention on the possible negative effects of program involvement. Under what conditions, for instance, might a program undermine a parent's sense of self-confidence (Hess, 1980) and prove to be a generally unproductive experience? The notion that parents can benefit from any type of intervention should be replaced with a healthy degree of ethical caution about the imposition of program values and methods on parents.

A better understanding of the processes of change in parents is necessary. How do parents deal with information that conflicts with their understandings of child development and perception of their child (Powell 1984a)? What program practices enhance parents' receptivity to innovative ideas and enable parents to change their belief systems and behaviors? In light of the growing emphasis on providing social support in parent initiatives, the role of social support in the adoption of new information also needs to be examined.

The limited amount of research on parental change processes reflects a general tendency in child development research to give minimal attention to the complexities of parental functioning. Parke (1978) has been particularly articulate in pointing out that developmentalists have gone to great lengths to understand children's cognitive processes but typically attribute little cognitive functioning to their parents. In recent years there has been a marked growth in research on parental belief systems (e.g., Sigel, 1985)

The need for experimental program development work regarding family-program interconnections offers an excellent context for collaborative enterprises between researchers and practitioners.

which has demonstrated, among other things, that parents hold a variety of beliefs about children and parenting (for a recent review, see Miller, 1988). Research on parent programs could contribute to this growing area of investigation. Goodnow (1988) has demonstrated how models and methods in social psychology can be used to benefit research on parents' ideas: Which particular ideas of parents are most open to change? Who seeks new information and under what conditions? How do people seek information? What forms of bias are displayed in the processing of information?

Opportunities and challenges

Changes in the structure and function of American families have precipitated profound growth and change in the field of early childhood education. Traditional program assumptions and practices regarding families have been called into question, and widespread interest in initiatives to enhance the family's childrearing role has soared. Once again, child and family issues are prominent on local, state, and national agendas.

For scholars interested in children and families, this is an opportune time to pursue important research questions, and for research findings to have impact on program design and delivery. Lessons have been learned from efforts to study early intervention, child care, and parent programs in the 1960s and 1970s. Consequently, research methodology has become more sophisticated in the past two decades, with corresponding maturity in the conceptualization of research problems. The questions require the expertise of a variety of disciplines; the territory is ripe for multidisciplinary investigations. Moreover, the historic gulf between researchers and practitioners has narrowed considerably in recent years (Almy, 1986), and the need for experimental program development work regarding family-program interconnections offers an excellent context for collaborative enterprises involving researchers and practitioners.

It remains to be seen whether adequate financial resources will be available for needed research and program development activities. In addition to research funds, support systems are required for facilitating communication among researchers and practitioners regarding program innovations and investigations. The serious interest and support of the nation's philanthropic foundations and government agencies will be essential to both small- and large-scale research and program development efforts.

Perhaps the greatest challenge is to transcend research and program service traditions that perpetuate a decontextualized and fragmented view of children and families. The distinction between child care and early education has historical antecedents, but in the present era serves to create somewhat false and divisive dichotomies (Scarr & Weinberg, 1986). Similarly, separating child care needs from other aspects of family functioning runs contrary to reality. A high-quality child care arrangement is one of the most important family-support systems of working parents (Powell, 1987b). Programmatic acknowledgment of the interdependencies of individual and family well-being is essential in an era where relations between the family and other institutions of society are being redefined.

References

Adams, D. (1976). *Parent involvement: Parent development.* Berkeley, CA: Center for the Study of Parent Involvement.

Almy, M. (1982). Day care and early childhood education. In E. F. Zigler & E. W. Gordon (Eds.), *Day care: Scientific and social policy issues* (pp. 476–496). Boston: Auburn House.

Almy, M. (1986). The past, present and future for the early childhood education researcher. *Early Childhood Research Quarterly, 1,* 1–13.

Anastasiow, N. (1988). Should parenting education be mandatory? *Topics in Early Childhood Special Education, 8*(1), 60–72.

Anchor, K., & Thomason, T. C. (1977). A comparison of two parent-training models with educated parents. *Journal of Community Psychology, 5,* 134–141.

Andrews, S. R., Blumenthal, J. B., Johnson, D. L., Kahn, A. J., Ferguson, C. J., Lasater, R. M., Malone, P. E., & Wallace, D. B. (1982). The skills of mothering: A study of Parent Child Development Centers. *Monographs of the Society for Research in Child Development, 47*(6, Serial No. 198).

Atkinson, A. M. (1987). A comparison of mothers' and providers' preferences and evaluations of day care center services. *Child and Youth Care Quarterly, 16,* 35–47.

Balaban, N. (1985). *Starting school: From separation to independence.* New York: Teachers College Press, Columbia University.

Baratz, S. S., & Baratz, J. C. (1970). Early childhood intervention: The social science base of institutional racism. *Harvard Educational Review, 40,* 29–50.

Beattie, N. (1985). *Professional parents.* Philadelphia: Falmer Press.

Becker, H. J., & Epstein, J. L. (1982). Parent involvement: A study of teacher practices. *Elementary School Journal, 83,* 85–102.

Bell, T. (1975). The child's right to have a trained parent. *Elementary School Guidance and Counseling, 9,* 271.

Belsky, J. (1988). The "effects" of infant day care reconsidered. *Early Childhood Research Quarterly, 3,* 235–272.

Biber, B. (1977). A developmental-interaction approach: Bank Street College of Education. In M. C. Day & R. K. Parker (Eds.), *The preschool in action* (2nd ed., pp. 423–460). Boston: Allyn & Bacon.

Blatchford, P., Battle, S., & Mays, J. (1982). *The first transition: Home to pre-school.* Windsor, Berkshire, Great Britain: NFER-Nelson Publishing Company.

Bogat, G. A., & Gensheimer, L. K. (1986). Discrepancies between the attitudes and actions of parents choosing day care. *Child Care Quarterly, 15,* 159–169.

Bradbard, M., & Endsley, R. (1980). The importance of educating parents to be discriminating day care consumers. In S. Kilmer (Ed.), *Advances in early education and day care* (Vol. 1, pp. 187–201). Greenwich, CT: JAI Press.

Bradbard, M. R., Endsley, R. C., & Readdick, C. A. (1983). How and why parents select profit-making day care programs: A study of two southeastern college communities. *Child Care Quarterly, 12,* 160–169.

123

Bridgeman, B., Blumenthal, J., & Andrews, S. (1981). *Parent Child Development Center: Final evaluation report. Report to Department of Health and Human Services.* Princeton, NJ: Educational Testing Service.

Brim, O. G. (1959). *Education for child rearing.* New York: Russell Sage.

Bronfenbrenner, U. (1974). *Is early intervention effective? A report on longitudinal evaluations of preschool programs* (Vol. 2). Washington, DC: Department of Health, Education and Welfare, Office of Child Development.

Bronfenbrenner, U. (1978). Who needs parent education? *Teachers College Record, 79,* 767–787.

Bronfenbrenner, U. (1979). *The ecology of human development: Experiments by nature and design.* Cambridge, MA: Harvard University Press.

Caldwell, B. M. (1980). Balancing children's rights and parent's rights. In R. Haskins & J. J. Gallagher (Eds.), *Care and education of young children in America* (pp. 27–50). Norwood, NJ: Ablex.

Caldwell, B. (1985). What is quality child care? In B. Caldwell & A. Hilliard (Eds.), *What is quality child care?* (pp. 1–16). Washington, DC: NAEYC.

Campbell, D. T. (1987). Problems in the experimenting society in the interface between evaluation and service providers. In S. L. Kagan, D. R. Powell, B. Weissbourd, & E. F. Zigler (Eds.), *America's family support programs: Perspectives and prospects* (pp. 345–351). New Haven, CT: Yale University Press.

Casto, G., & Mastropieri, M. A. (1986). The efficacy of early intervention programs: A meta-analysis. *Exceptional Children, 52,* 417–424.

Chilman, C. S. (1973). Programs for disadvantaged parents. In B. M. Caldwell & H. N. Ricciuti (Eds.), *Review of child development research* (Vol. 3, pp. 403–465). Chicago: University of Chicago Press.

Clarke-Stewart, K. A. (1984). Day care: A new context for research and development. In M. Perlmutter (Ed.), *The Minnesota Symposium on Child Psychology* (Vol. 17, pp. 917–1000). New York: Wiley.

Clarke-Stewart, K. A. (1987). Predicting child development from child care forms and features: The Chicago Study. In D. A. Phillips (Ed.), *Quality in child care: What does research tell us?* (pp. 1–19). Washington, DC: NAEYC.

Clarke-Stewart, K. A. (1988). Evolving issues in early childhood education: A personal perspective. *Early Childhood Research Quarterly, 3,* 139–149.

Clarke-Stewart, K. A., & Apfel, N. (1978). Evaluating parental effects on child development. In L. S. Shulman (Ed.), *Review of research in education* (pp. 47–119). Itasca, IL: Peacock.

Clarke-Stewart, K. A., & Fein, G. (1983). Early childhood programs. In M. M. Haith & J. J. Campos (Eds.), P. H. Mussen (Series Ed.), *Handbook of child psychology: Vol. 2. Infancy and development psychobiology* (pp. 917–1000). New York: Wiley.

Cochran, M. (1988a). Parental empowerment in family matters: Lessons learned from a research program. In D. R. Powell (Ed.), *Parent education as early childhood intervention* (pp. 23–50). Norwood, NJ: Ablex.

Cochran, M. (1988b). Generic issues in parent empowerment programs: A rejoinder to Mindick. In D. R. Powell (Ed.), *Parent education as early childhood intervention* (pp. 67–78). Norwood, NJ: Ablex.

Cochran, M., & Henderson, C. (1985). *Family matters: Evaluation of the parental empowerment program. Final report to the National Institute of Education.* Ithaca, NY: Cornell University.

Coelen, C., Glantz, F., & Calore, D. (1979). *Day care centers in the U.S.* Cambridge, MA: Abt Associates.

Coleman, J. S. (1987). Families and schools. *Educational Researcher, 16,* 32–38.

Coleman, J. S., Campbell, E. Q., Hobson, C. J., McPartland, J., Mood, A. M., Weinfeld, F. D., & York, R. L. (1966). *Equality of educational opportunity.* Washington, DC: U.S. Government Printing Office.

Coons, J. E., & Sugarman, S. D. (1978). *Education by choice: The case for family control.* Berkeley: The University of California Press.

Cowen, E. L., Gester, E. L., Boike, M., Norton, P., Wilson, A. B., & DeStefano, M. A. (1979). Hairdressers as caregivers: A descriptive profile of interpersonal help-giving involvements. *American Journal of Community Psychology, 9,* 715–729.

Cummings, E. H. (1980). Caregiver stability and day care. *Developmental Psychology, 16,* 31–37.

Deann, C. (1983). *Cooperative communication between home and school.* Ithaca, NY: Cornell University Media Services.

Dembo, M., Sweitzer, M., & Lauritzen, P. (1985). An evaluation of group parent education: Behavioral, PET, and Adlerian programs. *Review of Educational Research, 55,* 155–200.

Dickie, J. R., & Gerber, S. C. (1980). Training in social competence: The effect on mothers, fathers, and infants. *Child Development, 51,* 1248–1251.

Dokecki, P., Hargrove, E., & Sandler, H. (1983). An overview of the Parent Child Development Center social experiment. In R. Haskins & D. Adams (Eds.), *Parent education and public policy* (pp. 80–111). Norwood, NJ: Ablex.

Dunst, C. J., & Trivette, C. M. (1988). A family systems model of early intervention with handicapped and developmentally at-risk children. In D. R. Powell (Ed.), *Parent education as early childhood intervention* (pp. 131–179). Norwood, NJ: Ablex.

Eisenstadt, J., & Powell, D. (1987). Processes of participation in a mother-infant program as modified by stress and impulse control. *Journal of Applied Developmental Psychology, 8,* 17–37.

Elardo, R., & Caldwell, B. M. (1973). Value imposition in early education: Fact or fancy? *Child Care Quarterly, 2,* 6–13.

Ellwood, A. (1988). Prove to me that MELD makes a difference. In H. B. Weiss & F. H. Jacobs (Eds.), *Evaluating family programs* (pp. 303–313). Hawthorne, NY: Aldine de Gruyter.

Emlen, A. C., Donoghue, B. A., & LaForge, R. (1971). *Child care by kith: A study of the family day care relationships of working mothers and neighborhood caregivers. A report to Extramural Research and Demonstration Grants Branch, Children's Bureau, U.S. Department of Health, Education and Welfare.* Portland, OR: Portland State University.

Endsley, R. C., Bradbard, M. R., & Readdick, C. A. (1984). High-quality proprietary day care: Predictors of parents' choices. *Journal of Family Issues, 5,* 131–152.

Epstein, A. S., & Weikart, D. P. (1979). *The Ypsilanti-Carnegie Infant Education Project: Longitudinal follow-up.* (Monographs of the High/Scope Educational Research Foundation No. 6). Ypsilanti, MI: High/Scope Press.

Epstein, J. L. (1984a). School policy and parent involvement: Research results. *Educational Horizons, 62,* 70–72.

Epstein, J. L. (1984b). *Single parents and the schools: The effect of marital status on parent and teacher evaluations* (Report 353). Baltimore, MD: Center for Social Organization of Schools, The Johns Hopkins University.

Epstein, J. L. (1985). Home and school connections in schools of the future: Implications of research on parent involvement. *Peabody Journal of Education, 62,* 18–41.

Epstein, J. L. (1986). Parents' reactions to teacher practices of parent involvement. *Elementary School Journal, 86,* 277–293.

Epstein, J. L. (in press). Effects on student achievement of teachers' practices of parental involvement. In S. Silvern (Ed.), *Literacy through family, community and school interaction.* Greenwich, CT: JAI Press.

Epstein, J. L., & Becker, H. J. (1982). Teacher practices of parent involvement: Problems and possibilities. *Elementary School Journal, 83,* 103–113.

Family Resource Coalition. (1981). *Statement of philosophy, goals, and structure.* Chicago: Author.

Feeney, S., & Sysko, L. (1986). Professional ethics in early childhood education: Survey results. *Young Children, 42*(1), 15–20.

Fein, G. (1980). The informed parent. In S. Kilmer (Ed.), *Advances in early education and day care* (Vol. 1, pp. 155–185). Greenwich, CT: JAI Press.

Fein, G., & Clarke-Stewart, K. A. (1973). *Day care in context.* New York: Wiley.

Field, T., Gewirtz, J. L., Cohen, D., Garcia, R., Greenberg, R., & Collins, K. (1984). Leave-takings and reunions of infants, toddlers, preschoolers, and their parents. *Child Development, 55,* 628–635.

Fillmore, L. W. (1988, August). *Now or later? Issues related to the early education of minority group children.* Paper presented at the summer meeting of the Council of Chief State School Officers, Boston.

Frazier, F., & Matthews, W. A. (1975). Parent education: A comparison of Adlerian and behavioral approaches. *Elementary School Counseling and Guidance, 11,* 31–38.

Freeman, C. (1975). Adlerian mother study groups: Effects on attitudes and behavior. *Journal of Individual Psychology, 31,* 37–50.

Freud, A. (1952). The role of the teacher. *Harvard Educational Review, 22,* 229–235.

Fuqua, R. W., & Labensohn, D. (1986). Parents as consumers of child care. *Family Relations, 35,* 295–303.

Galinsky, E. (1981). *Between generations: The six stages of parenthood.* New York: Times Books.

Galinsky, E. (1986). Family life and corporate policies. In M. W. Yogman & T. B. Brazelton (Eds.), *In support of families* (pp. 109–145). Cambridge, MA: Harvard University Press.

Galinsky, E. (1988). Parents and teacher-caregivers: Sources of tension, sources of support. *Young Children, 43*(3), 4–12.

Galinsky, E., & Hooks, W. (1977). *The new extended family: Day care that works.* New York: Houghton Mifflin.

Gerson, M., Alpert, J. L., & Richardson, M. (1984). Mothering: The view from psychological research. *Signs, 9,* 434–453.

Getzels, J. W. (1974). Socialization and education: A note on discontinuities. *Teachers College Record, 76,* 218–225.

Gewirtz, J. L. (1978). Social learning in early human development. In A. C.

Catania & T. A. Brigham (Eds.), *Handbook of applied behavior analysis* (pp. 105–141). New York: Irvington.

Goelman, H., & Pence, A. R. (1987a). Effects of child care, family, and individual characteristics on children's language development: The Victoria Day Care Research Project. In D. A. Phillips (Ed.), *Quality in child care: What does research tell us?* (pp. 89–104). Washington, DC: NAEYC.

Goelman, H., & Pence, A. R. (1987b). Some aspects of the relationships between family structure and child language development in three types of day care. In D. L. Peters & S. Kontos (Eds.), *Continuity and discontinuity of experience in child care* (pp. 129–146). Norwood, NJ: Ablex.

Goodnow, J. J. (1988). Parents' ideas, actions, and feelings: Models and methods from developmental and social psychology. *Child Development, 59,* 286–320.

Goodson, B., & Hess, R. (1975). *The effects of parent training programs on child performance and parent behavior.* Unpublished manuscript, Stanford University, School of Education, Stanford, CA.

Gottlieb, B. H. (Ed.). (1988). *Marshaling social support: Formats, processes, and effects.* Beverly Hills, CA: Sage.

Gray, S. W., & Ruttle, K. (1980). The family-oriented home visiting program: A longitudinal study. *Genetic Psychology Monographs, 102,* 299–316.

Gray, S. W., & Wandersman, L. P. (1980). The methodology of home-based intervention studies: Problems and promising strategies. *Child Development, 51,* 993–1009.

Greenberg, P. (1969). *The devil has slippery shoes: A biased biography of the Child Development Group of Mississippi.* New York: Macmillan.

Halpern, R. (1984). Home-based early intervention: Emerging purposes, intervention approaches, and evaluation strategies. *Infant Mental Health Journal, 5,* 206–220.

Halpern, R. (1987). Major social and demographic trends affecting young families: Implications for early childhood care and development. *Young Children, 42*(6), 34–40.

Halpern, R., & Larner, M. (1988). The design of family support programs in high-risk communities: Lessons from the Child Survival/Fair Start initiative. In D. R. Powell (Ed.), *Parent education as early childhood intervention* (pp. 181–207). Norwood, NJ: Ablex.

Head Start assessment. (1977). Washington, DC: U.S. Department of Health, Education, and Welfare, Region III.

Heath, S. B., & McLaughlin, M. W. (1987). A child resource policy: Moving beyond dependence on school and family. *Phi Delta Kappan, 68,* 576–580.

Heinicke, C. M., Beckwith, L., & Thompson, A. (1988). Early intervention in the family system: A framework and review. *Infant Mental Health Journal, 9,* 111–141.

Henderson, A. (1987). *The evidence continues to grow: Parent involvement improves student achievement.* Columbia, MD: National Committee for Citizens in Education.

Hess, R. D. (1980). Experts and amateurs: Some unintended consequences of parent education. In M. Fantini & R. Cardenas (Eds.), *Parenting in a multicultural society* (pp. 3–16). New York: Longman.

Hess, R. D., & Croft, D. J. (1981). *Teachers of young children* (3rd ed.). Boston: Houghton Mifflin.

Hess, R. D., Dickson, W. P., Price, G. G., & Leong, D. J. (1979). Some contrasts between mothers and preschool teachers in interaction with four-year-old children. *American Educational Research Journal, 16,* 307–316.

Hess, R. D., Price, G. G., Dickson, W. P., & Conroy, M. (1981). Different roles for mothers and teachers: Contrasting styles of child care. In S. Kilmer (Ed.), *Advances in early education and day care* (Vol. 2, pp. 1–28). Greenwich, CT: JAI Press.

Hill-Scott, K. (1987). The effects of subsidized, private, and unregulated child care on family functioning. In D. L. Peters & S. Kontos (Eds.), *Continuity and discontinuity of experience in child care* (pp. 147–167). Norwood, NJ: Ablex.

Hock, E. (1984). The transition to day care: Effects of maternal separation anxiety on infant adjustment. In R. C. Ainslie (Ed.), *The child and the day care setting* (pp. 183–203). New York: Praeger.

Hock, E., McBride, S., & Gnezda, M. T. (in press). Maternal separation anxiety: Mother-infant separation from the maternal perspective. *Child Development.*

Hock, E., DeMeis, D., & McBride, S. (1988). Maternal separation anxiety: Its role in the balance of employment and motherhood in mothers of infants. In A. Gottfried & A. Gottfried (Eds.), *Maternal employment and children's development* (pp. 191–229). New York: Plenum.

Honig, A. S. (1979). *Parent involvement in early childhood education* (2nd ed.). Washington, DC: NAEYC.

Honig, A. S. (1989). Quality infant/toddler caregiving: Are there magic recipes? *Young Children, 44*(4), 4–10.

Hood, K. E., & McHale, S. M. (1987). Sources of stability and change in early childhood. In D. L. Peters & S. Kontos (Eds.), *Continuity and discontinuity of experience in child care* (pp. 17–39). Norwood, NJ: Ablex.

Howes, C., Goldenberg, C., Golub, J., Lee, M., & Olenick, M. (1984, April). *Continuity in socialization experiences in home and day care.* Paper presented at the annual meeting of the American Educational Research Association, New Orleans.

Howes, C., & Olenick, M. (1986). Family and child care influences on toddler's compliance. *Child Development, 57,* 202–216.

Hughes, R. (1985). The informal help-giving of home and center childcare providers. *Family Relations, 34,* 359–366.

Hymes, J. L. (1953). *Effective home-school relations.* New York: Prentice-Hall.

Jencks, C., Smith, M., Acland, H., Bane, M. J., Cohen, D., Gintis, H., Heyns, B., & Michelson, S. (1972). *Inequality: A reassessment of the effect of family and schooling in America.* New York: Basic.

Jester, R. E., & Guinagh, B. J. (1983). The Gordon Parent Education Infant and Toddler Program. In the Consortium for Longitudinal Studies, *As the twig is bent: Lasting effects of preschool programs* (pp. 103–132). Hillsdale, NJ: Erlbaum.

Joffe, C. E. (1977). *Friendly intruders: Childcare professionals and family life.* Berkeley, CA: University of California Press.

Johnson, D. L., & Breckenridge, J. N. (1982). The Houston Parent-Child Development Center and the primary prevention of behavior problems in young children. *American Journal of Community Psychology, 10,* 305–316.

Kagan, S. L. (1987). Home-school linkages: History's legacy and the family support movement. In S. L. Kagan, D. R. Powell, B. Weissbourd, & E. F. Zigler

(Eds.), *America's family support programs: Perspectives and prospects* (pp. 161–181). New Haven, CT: Yale University Press.

Kagan, S. L., Powell, D. R., Weissbourd, B., & Zigler, E. F. (Eds.). (1987). *America's family support programs: Perspectives and prospects.* New Haven, CT: Yale University Press.

Katz, L. G. (1980). Mothering and teaching: Some significant distinctions. In L. G. Katz (Ed.), *Current topics in early childhood education* (Vol. 3, pp. 47–63). Norwood, NJ: Ablex.

Keniston, K., & Carnegie Council on Children. (1977). *All our children: The American family under pressure.* New York: Harcourt Brace Jovanovich.

Kessen, W. (1979). The American child and other cultural inventions. *American Psychologist, 34,* 815–820.

Kessen, W., Fein, G., Clarke-Stewart, A., & Starr, S. (1975). *Variations in home-based infant education: Language, play and social development. Final report to the Office of Child Development, U.S. Department of Health, Education and Welfare.* New Haven, CT: Yale University.

Klaus, R. A., & Gray, S. W. (1968). The Early Training Project for disadvantaged children. *Monographs of the Society for Research in Child Development, 33*(4, Serial No. 120).

Klein, D. C., & Ross, A. (1958). Kindergarten entry: A study of role transition. In M. Krugman (Ed.), *Orthopsychiatry and the school.* New York: American Orthopsychiatric Association.

Kohn, M. (1969). *Class and conformity: A study in values.* Homewood, IL: Dorsey.

Kontos, S. (1984). Congruence of parent and early childhood staff perceptions of parenting. *Parenting Studies, 1,* 5–10.

Kontos, S. (1987). The attitudinal context of family-day care relationships. In D. L. Peters & S. Kontos (Eds.), *Continuity and discontinuity of experience in child care* (pp. 91–113). Norwood, NJ: Ablex.

Kontos, S., & Dunn, L. (in press). Attitudes of caregivers, maternal experiences with day care, and children's development. *Journal of Applied Developmental Psychology.*

Kontos, S., Raikes, H., & Woods, A. (1983). Early childhood staff attitudes toward their parent clientele. *Child Care Quarterly, 12,* 45–58.

Kontos, S., & Wells, W. (1986). Attitudes of caregivers and the day care experiences of families. *Early Childhood Research Quarterly, 1,* 47–67.

Lally, J. R., Mangione, P. L., & Honig, A. S. (1988). The Syracuse University Family Development Research Program: Long-range impact of an early intervention with low-income children and their families. In D. R. Powell (Ed.), *Parent education as early childhood intervention* (pp. 79–104). Norwood, NJ: Ablex.

Lambie, D. Z., Bond, J. T., & Weikart, D. P. (1974). *Home teaching with mothers and infants.* (Monographs of the High/Scope Educational Research Foundation No. 2). Ypsilanti, MI: High/Scope Press.

Laosa, L. (1979). Social competence in childhood: Toward a developmental, socioculturally relativistic paradigm. In M. W. Kent & J. E. Rolf (Eds.), *Primary prevention of psychopathology: Vol. 3. Social competence in children.* Hanover, NH: University Press of New England.

Laosa, L. (1980). Maternal teaching strategies in Chicano and Anglo-American families: The influence of culture and education on maternal behavior. *Child Development, 51,* 759–765.

Laosa, L. (1982). School, occupation, culture, and family: The impact of parental schooling on the parent-child relationship. *Journal of Educational Psychology, 74,* 791–827.

Larner, M., & Halpern, R. (1987). Lay home visiting: Strengths, tensions, and challenges. *Zero to Three, 8*(1), 1–7.

Larner, M., Nagy, C., & Halpern, R. (1987, October). *Inside the black box: Understanding home visiting programs.* Paper presented at the annual meeting of the American Public Health Association, New Orleans.

Lasch, C. (1977). *Haven in a heartless world: The family besieged.* New York: Basic.

Lazar, I., & Darlington, R. (1982). Lasting effects of early education: A report from the Consortium for Longitudinal Studies. *Monographs of the Society for Research in Child Development, 47*(2–3, Serial No. 195).

Levenstein, P. (1977). The Mother-Child Home Program. In M. C. Day & R. K. Parker (Eds.), *The preschool in action* (pp. 27–49). Boston: Allyn & Bacon.

Levenstein, P. (1988). *Messages from the home: The Mother-Child Home Program and the prevention of school disadvantage.* Columbus: Ohio State University Press.

Levenstein, P. (1989). Which homes? A response to Scarr and McCartney (1988). *Child Development, 60,* 514–516.

Levenstein, P., O'Hara, J., & Madden, J. (1983). The Mother-Child Home Program of the Verbal Interaction Project. In Consortium for Longitudinal Studies, *As the twig is bent: Lasting effects of preschool programs* (pp. 237–263). Hillsdale, NJ: Erlbaum.

Levine, J. A. (1982). The prospects and dilemmas of child care information and referral. In E. F. Zigler & E. W. Gordon (Eds.), *Day care: Scientific and social policy issues* (pp. 378–401). Boston: Auburn House.

Lightfoot, S. L. (1978). *Worlds apart: Relationships between families and schools.* New York: Basic.

Lippitt, R. (1968). Improving the socialization process. In J. A. Clausen (Ed.), *Socialization and society* (pp. 321–374). Boston: Little, Brown.

Litwak, E., & Meyer, H. (1974). *School, family and neighborhood: The theory and practice of school-community relations.* New York: Columbia University Press.

Lochman, J. E., & Brown, M. V. (1980). Evaluation of dropout clients and of perceived usefulness of a parent education program. *Journal of Community Psychology, 8,* 132–139.

Long, F., & Garduque, L. (1987). Continuity between home and family day care: Caregivers' and mothers' perceptions and children's social experiences. In D. L. Peters & S. Kontos (Eds.), *Continuity and discontinuity of experience in child care* (p. 69–90). Norwood, NJ: Ablex.

Lortie, D. (1975). *School teacher.* Chicago: University of Chicago Press.

Madden, J., Levenstein, P., & Levenstein, S. (1976). Longitudinal IQ outcomes of the Mother-Child Home Program. *Child Development, 47,* 1015–1025.

Madden, J., O'Hara, J., & Levenstein, P. (1984). Home again: Effects of the Mother-Child Home Programs on mother and child. *Child Development, 55,* 636–647.

Mann, M. B., & Thornburg, K. R. (1987). Guilt of working women with infants and toddlers in day care. *Early Child Development and Care, 27,* 451–464.

Maxima Corporation. (1983). *Project Head Start 1982–1983: Annual program information report.* Bethesda, MD: Author.

McBride, B. A. (1988). *The effects of a parent education/play group program on father involvement in childrearing*. Unpublished doctoral dissertation, University of Maryland, College Park.

McCartney, K., & Phillips, D. (1988). Motherhood and child care. In B. Birns & D. F. Hay (Eds.), *The different faces of motherhood* (pp. 157–183). New York: Plenum.

McCartney, K., & Scarr, S. (1989). Far from the point: A reply to Levenstein. *Child Development, 60,* 517–518.

McGuire, J. C., & Gottlieb, B. H. (1979). Social support groups among new parents: An experimental study in primary prevention. *Journal of Clinical Child Psychology, 8,* 111–116.

McIntosh, J. C. (1977). The first year of experience: Influence on beginning teachers (Doctorial dissertation, University of Toronto, 1976). *Dissertation Abstracts International, 38,* 3192–3193.

McKey, R. H., Condelli, L., Ganson, H., Barrett, B. J., McConkey, C., & Plantz, M. C. (1985). *The impact of Head Start on children, families and communities* (DHHS Publication No. 85-31193). Washington, DC: CSR Inc.

Meleen, P. J., Love, J. M., & Nauta, M. J. (1988). *Study of the home-based option in Head Start (Vol. 1). Submitted to the Administration for Children, Youth and Families, U.S. Department of Health and Human Services.* Hampton, NH: RMC Research Corporation.

Melson, G. F. (in press). The development of metasocialization: A theoretical framework. *Journal of Applied Developmental Psychology.*

Midco Educational Associates, Inc. (1972). *Investigation of the effects of parent participation in Head Start. Final technical report.* Denver, CO: Author.

Miller, S. A. (1988). Parents' beliefs about children's development. *Child Development, 59,* 259–285.

Moore, E. K., & McKinley, M. K. (1972). Parent involvement/control in child development programs. In D. N. McFadden (Ed.), *Early childhood development programs and services: Planning for action* (pp. 77–82). Washington, DC: NAEYC.

National Academy of Early Childhood Programs. (1984). *Accreditation criteria and procedures of the National Academy of Early Childhood Programs.* Washington, DC: NAEYC.

National Black Child Development Institute. (1987). *Safeguards: Guidelines for establishing programs for four-year-olds in the public schools.* Washington, DC: Author.

New York City Mayor's Office of Early Childhood Education. (1987–88). *Project Giant Step: General information and program requirements.* New York: Author.

Nixon, R. (1971, December 10). Text of veto message of Comprehensive Child Development Act of 1971. *Congressional Record,* pp. S21129–S21130.

O'Keefe, R. A. (1979). What Head Start means to families. In L. G. Katz (Ed.), *Current topics in early childhood education* (Vol. 2, pp. 43–67). Norwood, NJ: Ablex.

Olmsted, P. P., & Rubin, R. I. (1983). Parent involvement: Perspectives from the Follow Through experiment. In R. Haskins & D. Adams (Eds.), *Parent education and public policy* (pp. 112–140). Norwood, NJ: Ablex.

Palkovitz, R. (1987). Consistency and stability in the family microsystem environment. In D. L. Peters & S. Kontos (Eds.), *Continuity and discontinuity of .experience in child care* (pp. 41–67). Norwood, NJ: Ablex.

Parke, R.D. (1978). Parent-infant interaction: Progress, paradigms, and problems. In G. P. Sackett (Ed.), *Observing behavior* (Vol. 1, pp. 69–94). Baltimore, MD: University Park Press.

Parker, F. L., Piotrkowski, C. S., & Peay, L. (1987). Head Start as a social support for mothers: The psychological benefits of involvement. *American Journal of Orthopsychiatry, 57,* 220–233.

Pence, A. R., & Goelman, H. (1987). Silent partners: Parents of children in three types of day care. *Early Childhood Research Quarterly, 2,* 103–118.

Pestalozzi, J. (1951). *The education of man* (H. Gordon & R. Gordon, Trans.). New York: Philosophical Library.

Peters, D. L., & Kontos, S. (1987). Continuity and discontinuity of experience: An intervention perspective. In D. L. Peters & S. Kontos (Eds.), *Continuity and discontinuity of experience in child care* (pp. 1–16). Norwood, NJ: Ablex.

Phillips, D. A. (Ed.). (1987). *Quality in child care: What does research tell us?* Washington, DC: NAEYC.

Phillips, D. A., Scarr, S., & McCartney, K. (1987). Dimensions and effects of child care quality: The Bermuda study. In D. A. Phillips (Ed.), *Quality in child care: What does research tell us?* (pp. 43–56). Washington, DC: NAEYC.

Pinsker, M., & Geoffrey, K. (1981). Comparisons of parent effectiveness training and behavior modification parent training. *Family Relations, 30,* 61–68.

Powell, D. R. (1977). *Day care and the family: A study of interactions and congruence. Final technical report.* Detroit, MI: The Merrill-Palmer Institute.

Powell, D. R. (1978a). Correlates of parent-teacher communication frequency and diversity. *Journal of Educational Research, 71,* 333–343.

Powell, D. R. (1978b). The interpersonal relationship between parents and caregivers in day care settings. *American Journal of Orthopsychiatry, 48,* 680–689.

Powell, D. R. (1982). From child to parent: Changing conceptions of early childhood intervention. *Annals of the American Academy of Political and Social Science, 461,* 135–144.

Powell, D. R. (1983). Individual differences in participation in a parent-child support program. In I. Sigel & L. Laosa (Eds.), *Changing families* (pp. 203–224). New York: Plenum.

Powell, D. R. (1984a). Enhancing the effectiveness of parent education: An analysis of program assumptions. In L. Katz (Ed.), *Current topics in early childhood education* (Vol. 5, pp. 121–139). Norwood, NJ: Ablex.

Powell, D. R. (1984b). Social network and demographic predictors of length of participation in a parent education program. *Journal of Community Psychology, 12,* 13–20.

Powell, D. R. (1985). Stability and change in patterns of participation in a parent-child program. *Professional Psychology: Research and Practice, 16,* 172–180.

Powell, D. R. (1987a). Conceptual and methodological issues in research. In S. L. Kagan, D. R. Powell, B. Weissbourd, & E. Zigler (Eds.), *America's family support programs: Perspectives and prospects* (pp. 311–328). New Haven, CT: Yale University Press.

Powell, D. R. (1987b). Day care as a family support system. In S. L. Kagan, D. R. Powell, B. Weissbourd, & E. F. Zigler (Eds.), *America's family support programs: Perspectives and prospects* (pp. 115–132). New Haven, CT: Yale University Press.

Powell, D. R. (1987c). A neighborhood approach to parent support groups. *Journal of Community Psychology, 15,* 51–62.

Powell, D. R. (1988a). Emerging directions in parent-child intervention. In D.R. Powell (Ed.), *Parent education as early childhood intervention* (pp. 1–22). Norwood, NJ: Ablex.

Powell, D. R. (Ed.). (1988b). *Parent education as early childhood intervention.* Norwood, NJ: Ablex.

Powell, D. R. (1988c, June). *Seeking dimensions of quality in family support programs.* Paper presented at the A. L. Mailman Family Foundation Symposium, White Plains, N.Y.

Powell, D. R. (1988d). Support groups for low-income mothers: Design considerations and patterns of participation. In B. Gottlieb (Ed.), *Marshaling social support: Formats, processes, and effects* (pp. 111–134). Beverly Hills, CA: Sage Publications.

Powell, D. R. (in press). Strategies and limits of responsiveness to families in early childhood initiatives. *Marriage and Family Review.*

Powell, D. R., & Eisenstadt, J. W. (1982). Parents' searches for child care and the design of information services. *Children and Youth Services Review, 4,* 223–253.

Powell, D. R., & Eisenstadt, J. W. (1988). Informal and formal conversations in parent discussion groups: An observational study. *Family Relations, 37,* 166–170.

Powell, D. R., & Stremmel, A. J. (1987). Managing relations with parents: Research notes on the teacher's role. In D. L. Peters & S. Kontos (Eds.), *Continuity and discontinuity of experience in child care* (pp. 115–127). Norwood, NJ: Ablex.

Powell, D. R., & Widdows, R. (1987). Social and economic factors associated with parents' decisions about after-school child care: An exploratory study in a medium-sized community. *Child and Youth Care Quarterly, 16,* 268–278.

Power, T. J. (1985). Perceptions of competence: How parents and teachers view each other. *Psychology in the Schools, 22,* 68–78.

Radin, N. (1972). Three degrees of maternal involvement in a preschool program: Impact on mothers and children. *Child Development, 43,* 1355–1364.

Ramey, C. T., Bryant, D. M., & Suarez, T. M. (1985). Preschool compensatory education and the modifiability of intelligence: A critical review. In D. Detterman (Ed.), *Current topics in human intelligence* (pp. 247–296). Norwood, NJ: Ablex.

Ramey, C., Dorval, B., & Baker-Ward, L. (1983). Group day care and socially disadvantaged families: Effects on the child and the family. In S. Kilmer (Ed.), *Advances in early education and day care* (Vol. 3, pp. 69–132). Greenwich, CT: JAI Press.

Ramirez, M., & Castaneda, A. (1974). *Cultural democracy, bicognitive development and education.* New York: Academic.

Reicken, H. W., & Boruch, R. F. (1974). *Social experimentation: A method for planning and evaluating social intervention.* New York: Academic.

Rheingold, H. (1973). To rear a child. *American Psychologist, 28,* 42–46.

Rich, D. (1985). *The forgotten factor in school success — The family.* Washington, DC: Home and School Institute.

Robinson, J. L., & Choper, W. B. (1979). Another perspective on program evaluation: The parents speak. In E. Zigler & J. Valentine (Eds.), *Project Head Start: A legacy of the War on Poverty* (pp. 467–476). New York: Free Press.

Rodriquez, G. G., & Cortez, C. P. (1988). The evaluation experience of the AVANCE Parent-Child Education Program. In H. B. Weiss & F. H. Jacobs

(Eds.), *Evaluating family programs* (pp. 287–301). Hawthorne, NY: Aldine de Gruyter.

Rogler, L. H., Malgady, R. G., Costantino, G., & Blumenthal, R. (1987). What do culturally sensitive mental health services mean? The case of Hispanics. *American Psychologist, 42,* 565–570.

Rubenstein, J. L., & Howes, C. (1979). Caregiving and infant behavior in day care and in homes. *Developmental Psychology, 15,* 1–24.

Scarr, S., & McCartney, K. (1988). Far from home: An experimental evaluation of the Mother-Child Home Program in Bermuda. *Child Development, 59,* 531–543.

Scarr, S., & Weinberg, R. A. (1986). The early childhood enterprise: Care and education of the young. *American Psychologist, 41,* 1140–1146.

Schofield, R. (1979). Parent group education and student self-esteem. *Social Work in Education, 1,* 26–33.

Schultz, T., & Lombardi, J. (1989). Right from the start: A report on the NASBE Task Force on Early Childhood Education. *Young Children, 44*(2), 6–10.

Schwarz, J. C., & Wynn, R. (1971). The effects of mothers' presence and previsits on children's emotional reaction to starting nursery school. *Child Development, 42,* 871–881.

Seitz, V. (1987). Outcome evaluation of family support programs: Research design alternatives to true experiments. In S. L. Kagan, D. R. Powell, B. Weissbourd, & E. F. Zigler (Eds.), *America's family support programs: Perspectives and prospects* (pp. 329–344). New Haven, CT: Yale University Press.

Seitz, V., Rosenbaum, L. K., & Apfel, N. (1985). Effects of family support intervention: A ten-year follow-up. *Child Development, 56,* 376–391.

Sigel, I. E. (Ed.). (1985). *Parental belief systems.* Hillsdale, NJ: Erlbaum.

Slaughter, D. T. (1983). Early intervention and its effects on maternal and child development. *Monographs of the Society for Research in Child Development, 48*(4, Serial No. 202).

Smelser, N. J. (1965). The social challenge to parental authority. In S. M. Farber, P. Mustacchi, & R. H. Wilson (Eds.), *Man and civilization: The family's search for survival* (pp. 67–72). New York: McGraw-Hill.

Smith, M. Brewster. (1968). Competence and socialization. In J. A. Clausen (Ed.). *Socialization and society* (pp. 270–320). Boston: Little, Brown.

Smith, Mildred B. (1968). School and home: Focus on achievement. In A. H. Passow (Ed.), *Developing programs for the educationally disadvantaged* (pp. 87–107). New York: Teachers College Press, Columbia University.

Stearns, M. S. (1971). *Report on preschool programs: The effects of preschool programs on disadvantaged children and their families. Final report.* Washington, DC: Department of Health, Education and Welfare, Office of Child Development.

Strain, P. S., & Smith, B. J. (1986). A counter-interpretation of early intervention effects: A response to Casto and Mastropieri. *Exceptional Children, 52,* 260–265.

Stubbs, J. L. (1980). *National Head Start Parent Involvement Study. Part I: Opportunities for parent involvement.* United Research and Development Corporation.

Tharp, R. G. (1982). The effective instruction of comprehension: Results and descriptions of the Kamehameha Early Education Program. *Reading Research Quarterly, 17,* 503–527.

Tharp, R. G. (1989). Psychocultural variables and constants: Effects on teaching and learning in schools. *American Psychologist, 44,* 349–359.

Tharp, R., & Gallimore, R. (1988). *Rousing minds to life: Teaching, learning, and schooling in social context.* Cambridge, England: Cambridge University Press.

Tharp, R. G., Jordan, C., Speidel, G., Au, K. H., Klein, T. W., Sloat, K. C. M., Calkins, R. P., & Gallimore, R. (1984). Product and process in applied developmental research: Education and the children of a minority. In M. E. Lamb, A. L. Brown, & B. Rogoff (Eds.), *Advances in developmental psychology* (Vol. 3, pp. 91–144). Hillsdale, NJ: Erlbaum.

Tizard, J., Schofield, W. N., & Hewison, J. (1982). Collaboration between teachers and parents in assisting children's reading. *British Journal of Educational Research, 52*(1), 1–11.

Travers, J., Nauta, M., & Irwin, N. (1982). *The effects of a social program: Final report of the Child and Family Resource Program's Infant-Toddler Component* (HHS-105-79-1301). Cambridge, MA: Abt Associates.

Valentine, J., & Stark, E. (1979). The social context of parent involvement in Head Start. In E. Zigler & J. Valentine (Eds.), *Project Head Start: A legacy of the War on Poverty* (pp. 291–313). New York: Free Press.

Veenman, S. (1984). Perceived problems of beginning teachers. *Review of Educational Research, 54,* 143–178.

Waller, W. (1932). *The sociology of teaching.* New York: Wiley.

Wandersman, L. P. (1987). New directions in parent education. In S. L. Kagan, D. R. Powell, B. Weissbourd, & E. F. Zigler (Eds.), *America's family support programs: Perspectives and prospects* (pp. 207–227). New Haven, CT: Yale University Press.

Wandersman, L. P., Wandersman, A., & Kahn, S. (1980). Social support in the transition to parenthood. *Journal of Community Psychology, 8,* 332–342.

Washington, V., & Oyemade, U. J. (1985). Changing family trends: Head Start must respond. *Young Children, 40*(6), 12–15, 17–18.

Weikart, D., Bond, J. T., & McNeil, J. (Eds.). (1978). *The Ypsilanti Perry Preschool Project: Preschool years and longitudinal results through fourth grade.* (Monographs of the High/Scope Educational Research Foundation No. 3). Ypsilanti, MI: High/Scope Educational Research Foundation.

Weinraub, M. (1977, March). *Children's responses to maternal absence: An experimental intervention study.* Paper presented at the biennial meeting of the Society for Research in Child Development, New Orleans.

Weinraub, M., & Frankel, J. (1977). Sex differences in parent-infant interaction during free play, departure and separation. *Child Development, 48,* 1240–1249.

Weinraub, M., & Lewis, M. (1977). The determinants of children's responses to brief periods of maternal absence. *Monographs of the Society for Research in Child Development, 42*(4, Serial No. 172).

Weiss, H. B. (1988). Family support and education programs: Working through ecological theories of human development. In H. B. Weiss & F. H. Jacobs (Eds.), *Evaluating family programs* (pp. 3–36). Hawthorne, NY: Aldine de Gruyter.

Weiss, H. B., & Jacobs, F. (Eds.). (1988). *Evaluating family support programs* (pp. 267–285). Hawthorne, NY: Aldine de Gruyter.

Weiss, H. B., & Seppanen, P. (1988). States and families: A new window of opportunity for family support and education programs. *Family Resource Coalition Report, 7*(3), 15–17.

Weissbourd, B. (1983). The family support movement: Greater than the sum of its parts. *Zero to Three, 4*(1), 8–10.

Weissbourd, B. (1987). A brief history of family support programs. In S. L. Kagan, D. R. Powell, B. Weissbourd, & E. F. Zigler (Eds.), *America's family support programs: Perspectives and prospects* (pp. 38–56). New Haven, CT: Yale University Press.

Winetsky, C. S. (1978). Comparisons of the expectations of parents and teachers for the behavior of preschool children. *Child Development, 49,* 1146–1154.

Winkelstein, E. (1981). Day care/family interaction and parental satisfaction. *Child Care Quarterly, 10,* 334–340.

Zigler, E., & Berman, W. (1983). Discerning the future of early childhood intervention. *American Psychologist, 38,* 894–906.

Zigler, E. F., & Freedman, J. (1987). Head Start: A pioneer of family support. In S. L. Kagan, D. R. Powell, B. Weissbourd, & E. F. Zigler (Eds.), *America's family support programs: Perspectives and prospects* (pp. 57–76). New Haven, CT: Yale University Press.

Zigler, E. F., & Turner, P. (1982). Parents and day care workers: A failed partnership? In E. F. Zigler & E. W. Gordon (Eds.), *Day care: Scientific and social policy issues* (pp. 174–182). New York: Free Press.

Index

By author

Information about NAEYC

NAEYC is . . .

. . . a membership-supported organization of people committed to fostering the growth and development of children from birth through age 8. Membership is open to all who share a desire to serve and act on behalf of the needs and rights of young children.

NAEYC provides . . .

. . . educational services and resources to adults who work with and for children, including
- *Young Children,* the journal for early childhood educators
- **Books, posters, brochures, and videos** to expand professional knowledge and commitment to young children, with topics including infants, curriculum, research, discipline, teacher education, and parent involvement
- An **Annual Conference** that brings people from all over the country to share their expertise and advocate on behalf of children and families
- **Week of the Young Child** celebrations sponsored by NAEYC Affiliate Groups across the nation to call public attention to the needs and rights of children and families
- **Insurance plans** for individuals and programs
- **Public affairs information** for knowledgeable advocacy efforts at all levels of government and through the media
- The **National Academy of Early Childhood Programs,** a voluntary accreditation system for high-quality programs for children
- The **Information Service,** a computerized, central source of information sharing, distribution, and collaboration

For free information about membership, publications, or other NAEYC services . . .

. . . call NAEYC at 202-232-8777 or 800-424-2460 or write to NAEYC, 1834 Connecticut Avenue, N.W., Washington, DC 20009-5786.